Tamura
Ryuichi

on the life and work
of a 20th century master

D0814411

Tamura Ryuichi

on the life and work
of a 20th century master

• • • • • • • • • • • • • • • • • •

Takako Lento & Wayne Miller, Editors

The Unsung Masters Series at Pleiades Press
Warrensburg, Missouri, 2011
• • • • • • • •

ISBN 978-0-9641454-2-9

Published by Pleiades Press
Department of English
The University of Central Missouri
Warrensburg, Missouri 64093

Distributed by Small Press Distribution (SPD)

Book design by Wayne Miller. Series design by Kevin Prufer.

2 4 6 8 9 7 5 3 1
First Pleiades Press Printing, 2011

Our profound thanks to Mrs. Tamura Etsuko for giving us the included images and for the permission to print Tamura's work. Also to Tom Lento for his insights, support, and careful line edits, to Christopher Drake for his generosity, to Kevin Prufer and Phong Nguyen for their consultation, and to Jeanne Ouellette for her patience.

Invaluable financial support for this project has been provided by the National Endowment for the Arts and the Missouri Arts Council, a state agency. Our immense gratitude to both organizations.

ART WORKS.
arts.gov

Missouri
Arts Council
The State of the Arts

Contents

Introduction

Wayne Miller

I first encountered Tamura Ryuichi's poetry in *The Vintage Book of Contemporary World Poetry*, where I found myself struck by the brilliance of the three Tamura poems included: "Every Morning after Killing Thousands of Angels," "My Imperialism," and "Human House."[1] The poems were dark and unflinching. They seemed both deeply personal and, at the same time, sharply engaged with political and historical concerns—a rare combination. All were in Christopher Drake's translation, so I went online to find a copy of *Dead Languages*, the book of Tamura's poems Drake had published with Katydid Books in 1984. Though Katydid's publisher has since set up a website making available back publications, at the time it was nearly impossible to find *Dead Languages*. The very few copies for sale were beaten up and cost at least $40.

When I opened my ragged copy I knew I was glad I'd spent the money. The additional poems were just as exciting as the Mc-Clatchy selections, and Drake's introduction was enlightening. Since you can read Drake's "Introduction to Dead Languages" later in

[1] "Human House" is titled "The House of Man" in Takako Lento's translation, the version included in this book.

this volume, I won't rehash most of its details, except to say that Tamura shares a lot with a number of poets of his transnational cohort. Tamura was born in 1923, and like many of his contemporaries, he was something of a political and cultural dissenter in the years leading up to World War II. In particular, amid the nationalist fervor of Japan's Imperial period, Tamura felt a deep connection with Western Modernist poetry, and he was particularly drawn to Eliot's *The Waste Land*, which was translated by Ayukawa Nobuo into Japanese in 1940. Tamura was also profoundly affected by his experiences during the war—in particular the experience of manning an artillery emplacement to defend against the American and Soviet invasion that never came. What's more, in the war's aftermath Tamura worked hard to re-imagine a new poetry—to account for how World War II had changed what poetry could and should be. Like Adorno, Tamura knew poetry presented a problem after the horrors of the war; like Celan, he knew that the period's propaganda had altered the nature of language and, thus, that language—particularly poetic language—needed to be reclaimed or reinvented for the future. Tamura approached these poetic, philosophical, and linguistic problems in conjunction with a loose group of Japanese poets called the "Wasteland" poets since they were partially inspired by Western Modernists such as Eliot and published the literary journal *Arechi* (*The Wasteland*) for a number of years.

My own locus as a poet and poetry reader is surely Western—I know little about the history or aesthetics of Japanese poetry—and it's a fair criticism of my ongoing interest in Tamura to say that I'm drawn to his poems at least partially because Tamura is international in scope and decidedly influenced by Western writers with which I'm familiar. Indeed, Tamura often intentionally subverts many traditional Japanese poetic conventions; for instance, he often uses the first person pronoun in his poems, something that's generally avoided in traditional Japanese poetry.

But what draws me most to Tamura's work is its difficult, stoic, and often paradoxical philosophical worldview. It could be said that Tamura's life was saved by the atomic destruction of Hiroshima and Nagasaki, for it's surely likely that he would have died if he'd been forced to defend Japan against an Allied invasion. Tamura's experience of waiting for the unknown to come and claim him, followed by his own salvation as the result of massive destruction elsewhere, links him to the absurd, unpredictably horrifying experiences of numerous European writers during the war—and, broadly speaking, to what is sometimes called "poetry of witness." (In fact, four poems by Tamura are included in Carolyn Forche's anthology *Against Forgetting*.) As such, he is part of the generation that witnessed firsthand the failures of Modernist systems of social organization and, furthermore, experienced on a personal level the terrible effects of those failures. Additionally, Tamura's grounding in Modernist poetics, coupled with his attention to the difficulties and slipperiness of language, makes him, like many of his contemporaries in Japan and elsewhere, a kind of bridge between Modernism and Postmodernism.

Tamura's dark and sometimes even brutal approach to the subjects of violence and survival resonates with the perspective of Czeslaw Milosz in the famous poem "Child of Europe," which begins with the horrifying, though perhaps necessary, survivor's assertion, "We, whose lungs fill with the sweetness of day, / Who in May admire trees flowering / Are better than those who perished."[2] Tamura's fugue-like repetition and reweaving in poems such as "Standing Coffin" and "World Without Words" suggest Paul Celan's traumatized tangle of memory and language in "Death Fugue." Tamura's socio-historical pessimism sounds like many of his European contemporaries—particularly Zbigniew Herbert and later Auden. And Tamura reminds me perhaps most directly of Tadeusz Rozewicz; both poets are skeptical of the traditional, culturally reinforcing role of the poet, which they attack through a self-reflexivity that has less to do with Postmodern "play" than with a deep concern that the poet will betray the narrow space (the "thin line") that remains for him to occupy in the wake of historical cataclysm. Rozewicz asserts that poems exist as occasional closings of one's eyes to realism and materialism; similarly, Tamura explains that silence is born "because an angel blocks time / above our heads." For Rozewicz, "contemporary poetry / is a fight for breath";[3] for Tamura, beautiful words are things that might "take revenge against you." For Rozewicz, a poet is "one who tries to

---

[2] Translated by Jan Darowski.
[3] From "Relieving the Burden," translated by Victor Contoski.

leave / and one who cannot leave";[4] for Tamura, a poem is "a kind of balance of terror."

Like those of many of his contemporaries, Tamura's poems often present the human condition as one of impossible choices, to which the best responses are paradoxical in nature. Thus, in the poem "Four Thousand Days and Nights" (which marks more or less the time elapsed between Japan's surrender and the 1956 publication of the poem in Tamura's first collection, also titled *Four Thousand Days and Nights*) we find a cruel paradox: for Tamura, poems require the destruction of "many we love"—their existences, our memories of them—and we eradicate them because it is the only way to "resurrect the dead," to memorialize them and move forward into the future. (As Milan Kudera says, "Remembering is a form of forgetting."[5]) In Tamura's poem "Standing Coffin" the closing couplet asserts, "we have no venom / we have no venom to heal us." Having followed our human impulses into the violence of war, there is no medicine to heal humanity in the war's aftermath; rather, from Tamura's perspective, we need a venom capable of attacking, and thus perhaps subduing, that part of us—individually, historically—that participated. In "The Man with a Green Face," Tamura speaks, again through paradox, to the question of how to move beyond the postwar period's cultural and artistic stagnation: "We need more cunning to kill our hunger / more imagination to end our dreaming." According to Tamura at the poem's end, perhaps the best we humans can hope for is a bit of sensory pleasure in the midst of our mortality and self-destruction—"is, on the tongues of gravediggers, the taste of ice cream."

The color green often appears in Tamura's poems, where it tends to embody a paradoxical duplicity: on the one hand, green is the color of rebirth and spring; on the other, green is the color of sickness and decay. Thus, in "Dead Leaves," Tamura avers that leaves die "without shedding green / blood," returning to "the color of the earth"; unlike humans, whose bodies turn green with rot if left unburied, leaves draw their vital greenness inward until it dis-

---

[4] From "Who Is a Poet," translated by Magnus Krynski and Robert McGuire.

[5] From *Testaments Betrayed*, trans. Linda Asher.

appears, which, according to Tamura, allows them to return more easily to the earth. In "The Man with a Green Face," as World War II fighter pilots "sail out of sight," never to return, the man sickened by the military display—"the man with a green face"—is the only one who "tries to break out of history." He is, in other words, sickened by the cultural hubris of the enormous historical events around him, which so easily draw others into their fold. In "Green Conceptual Body," the speaker finds himself sickened by the "conceptual bodies" in which people's thoughts run free, without skepticism. These are, as Kenneth Burke might say, the places where we are most clearly our human selves, yet, as Tamura puts it, where we also forge "the vertical nightmare of Medieval gothic, / the ascending nightmare knotting heaven and earth"—the nightmare of our own "hierarchical classes." In response to this realization, the speaker finds himself lying down in the grass (which, of course, is also green)—and thus "the horizontal / pushes through my conceptual body / the Gothic collapses." This "horizontalness" allows him to live in a present, individualized moment that includes neither the horror of grave digging nor the lofty corruptibility of abstract ideas. The value of poetry for Tamura is similar: it makes "humans close their eyes, / stretch out their arms, stand precisely there."

Like Hannah Arendt, Tamura holds up an unflagging attention to the individual—and particularly the individual fully present in the present world before him—as an antidote to the kinds of totalizing abstractions that allowed for—and resulted from—a destructive nationalism. Tamura closes "The House of Man" by asserting, defiantly:

> my idea of going home is not based on political belief or
>   religious creed
> I just want to see with my own eyes
> the collapse of the house of man
> the deconstruction of my language
>
> of course my house is not made of your words
> my house is made of my words

For Tamura, each of us has his/her own private language through which (s)he explains the world, and attending to the details of that world without organizing them in a hierarchy is essential to avoiding the pitfalls of abstract conceptualizing. As such, to borrow language from "Green Conceptual Body," Tamura privileges the "horizontal" position over the "vertical"—the level and equal over the hierarchical. Yet, it's also true that "horizontal" is the position of the dead. The living, by virtue of their human nature, have no choice but to stand up into the "vertical" if they are to live. Thus, Tamura's view of the individual is finally, like many of his views, paradoxical: the individual is something to be attended to with care and, at the same time, treated with skepticism, since (s)he can only partially avoid the pitfalls of history.

Perhaps for this reason, Tamura spends quite a bit of time in his poems debasing or attacking birds, those creatures that so often attracted the Romantic poetic imagination. (For Tamura, they are often overlaid with images of fighter aircraft.) In "Four Thousand Days and Nights," the speaker and his fellow poets shoot down "the silence of four thousand nights and the backlight of four thousand days / simply because [they] wanted the trembling tongue of a single small bird"—a grotesque symbol, perhaps, of poetry. In "A Visionary," we find the sky adrift with wreckage, including "a small bird" which "must pass through our bitter hearts / to return to its nest." In "Green Conceptual Body," "birds fly inside birds nailed to the sky" and humans "can't fly like birds / so they put wings on concepts / to feel the pleasure of crashing." For Tamura, as for the Romantics, birds represent a kind of lofty, superhuman striving toward transcendence—yet Tamura, from his postwar 20th century vantage, sees such striving as artificial and dangerous, resulting in crashes—personal, cultural, and historical. For Tamura, the idealized bird is a cautionary symbol.

These are just a few quick observations about Tamura's poetry. What I ultimately find most compelling about the poems themselves is how, thanks to Tamura's complex thinking and his unique and haunting attention to image, they keep opening as I continue to revisit them. I'm fascinated by the ways his poems interact with the ideas and works of numerous 20th century poets from a range of countries and cultures. And, observed from my own 21st century vantage, Tamura continues to speak profoundly to the world's intensifying modernity as we push forward into history. He's deeply aware of the difficult and unstable place of the individual inside our complex sociopolitical matrices, and he's wary of the poet's role as (s)he speaks into such a complicated context. What's more, he's also very aware that Total War is modernity's grandest and most terrifying invention—something that informs his view of society, modern Man, and, more disturbingly, himself, since he, too, is modern Man.

For all these reasons, when in 2009 we at Pleiades Press got an NEA grant to expand Kevin Prufer's and D. A. Powell's Unsung Masters feature on Dunstan Thompson to a book-length format, I decided that, if the opportunity presented itself, I'd focus my own subsequent volume on Tamura. When the second grant came through, however, it became quickly clear that I couldn't undertake such a project alone. Despite my appreciation for Tamura's poems, my knowledge of Japanese poetry was extremely limited, not to mention that I spoke no Japanese. How would I handle rights issues? How would I find Japanese perspectives on Tamura's work? How would I know if Drake's translations were faithful enough to represent Tamura? I had a lot of important questions and no one, really, to turn to. I attempted to track down Christopher Drake, but at that point all my efforts proved fruitless. (It wasn't until more than a year later, in 2010, that I finally got in touch with him to get permission to reprint the included portions of his fine work on Tamura.)

Thus, it was serendipity when right about that time Poetry International Web published several Tamura poems, translated by Takako Lento. The translations read extraordinarily well and a couple overlapped with Drake's, indicating that both Drake's and Lento's were strong and faithful. I quickly got in touch with Ms. Lento. When I explained the project I was hoping to embark on, she jumped on board—and thus our editorial collaboration began.

In fact, this project would have been impossible without her. It turns out Takako, who was born in Japan but has lived in the United States for more than 30 years, had known Tamura for decades. They were both members of the International Writing Program at the University of Iowa, though at different times. Moreover, Takako's husband, Tom Lento, was something of a drinking buddy of Tamura's. (Tamura is more than a little renowned for his love of whisky.) Takako had even published a small collection of Tamura's poems in translation (published by Ceres Press), and she knew from her days in Iowa Samuel Grolmes and Yumiko Tsumura,[6] two of Tamura's other translators. I had found exactly the person the project needed to move forward.

Our primary goal in *Tamura Ryuichi: On the Life & Work of a 20th Century Master* is to present to an American audience a selection of Tamura's poems and a series of essays that both contextualize and make a case for the importance of his work. While Tamura is little known in the U.S., he is considered in Japan to be among the most important 20th century poets. It's worth reiterating here that Tamura is to Japanese poetry more or less what Zbigniew Herbert or Tadeusz Rozewicz is to Polish poetry, what Celan is to German poetry. American poets born the same year as Tamura include Anthony Hecht, Richard Hugo, Denise Levertov, and James Schuyler, and he holds a similar standing to theirs, as well. Thus, Takako suggested she could find a number of interesting essays by Japanese critics on Tamura's work to include in this volume. From a larger group, we selected essays by fellow "Wasteland" poet Ayukawa Nobuo, prominent postwar poets Tanikawa Shuntaro and Ooka Makoto, and somewhat younger poet Yoshimasu Gozo,[7] who knew Tamura from Japan, succeeded him at Iowa in 1970-1, and spent time with him in both Iowa and New York when Tamura returned to the U.S. in 1971 for a reading tour. (Yoshimasu also introduced Tamura to contributor Laurence Lieberman the following year in Japan.) We chose these particular essays because we found them to be accessible to an American audience and to offer some context

---

[6] Though Grolmes and Tsumura's translations in their more-or-less self-published book, *Poetry of Ryuichi Tamura* (CCC Press, 1998), are quite capable, in the interest of simplicity we left them out of this volume.
[7] All names by Japanese authors are presented in traditional Japanese manner, with the surname first. Takako Lento's and Miho Nonaka's names, however, are presented in the Western manner, with surnames last.

and explanation for Tamura's work from a purely Japanese perspective.

We also wanted to include essays by American writers who might respond to Tamura's poetry from a Western perspective— or at least from a perspective that might not be quite as focused on the nuances of Japanese literature. Three of Tamura's American translators—Christopher Drake, Takako Lento, and Marianne Tarcov—have contributed essays as well as translations, and we've also included essays by Japanese-American poet Miho Nonaka and poet Laurence Lieberman, each of whom offers a unique vantage from which to view Tamura's work. Nonaka is a dual citizen who has published poetry (in Japanese) in Japan as well as (in English) in the U.S., where she is now a professor of writing and literature. Lieberman became friends with Tamura while on a Fulbright to Japan (introduced by Yoshimasu) and thus spent quite a bit of time getting to know him. In addition to giving us a sense of Tamura as a person in the context of his day-to-day life, Lieberman's essay also deals in part with his attempts to write "imitations" (à la Robert Lowell) of Tamura's poems.

Obviously, given the availability of Tamura criticism in Japan, there's a lot more we could have included. But our primary goal in this volume—and in the Unsung Masters Series in general—is really that of introducing underappreciated writers to an American audience, so in the interest of keeping your attention (please read on, read on!) we kept the book to a manageable length.

The first volume in the Unsung Masters Series focused on Dunstan Thompson—a clearly neglected American author. This volume expands the aims of the series, bringing into focus a poet of significant literary standing in his own country who, because of the vicissitudes of translation and publication, hasn't received the attention in this country he deserves. After all, many of the non-American poets who are well known in the U.S. are well known in part because a prominent poet or critic was there to advocate for their work. For example, think of the uniquely entangled relationship between American and Polish poetries facilitated in part by Czeslaw Milosz's and Adam Zagajewski's presence in the U.S. Or think of Charles Simic's advocacy for Serbian poets such as Novica Tadic and Vasko Popa. Our hope is that the Unsung Masters Series will do what it can to enlarge the audience for writers—American and non-American—who deserve more attention in the U.S. than they currently receive. In the case of Tamura, both Takako and I—as well as my fellow series editors Kevin Prufer and Phong Nguyen—hope you'll find his poems as wonderfully compelling as we do.

(2011)

A Folio of Poems by Tamura Ryuichi

Etching

He sees, in front of him, a landscape like one he saw in a German etching. It seems like a bird's-eye view of an ancient city, which is about to shift from evening into night, or like a realistic picture representing a modern precipice that is changing from deep night into daybreak.

He, namely the man I have begun to tell you about, killed his father when he was young. That autumn his mother went beautifully mad.

[trans. Takako Lento]

Four Thousand Days and Nights

In order for a poem to be born
we must kill
we must kill many
we shoot down, assassinate, poison many we love

Look,
from the skies of four thousand days and nights
we shot down
the silence of four thousand nights and the backlight of four thou-
     sand days
simply because we wanted the trembling tongue of a single small bird

Listen,
we assassinated
four thousand days of love and four thousand nights of pity
from all the rainy cities, blast-furnaces,
mid-summer wharfs, and coal mines
simply because we needed the tears of a single starved child

Remember,
we poisoned to kill
the imaginations of four thousand nights and the chilling memories
     of four thousand days
simply because we wanted the fears of one stray dog
who sees what our eyes do not see
who hears what our ears do not hear

In order to give birth to a poem
we must kill those we love
that is the only way to resurrect the dead
it is the path we must take

[trans. Takako Lento]

October Poem

In crisis you may know me
beneath my smooth skin
emotions break like hard rain
corpse after corpse is thrown up
on deserted October shores

   October is my empire
   my gentle hands rule what is being lost
   my small eyes watch what is disappearing
   my soft ears hear the silence of what is dying

Through fear you may know me
in my plentiful blood
flows a time of total murder
fresh hunger shivers
in October's cold sky

   October is my empire
   my dead troops occupy all the wet cities
   my dead pilots circle above missing minds
   my dead populace signs documents for those still dying

[trans. Christopher Drake]

Far Country

My pain
is a simple thing
    like feeding an animal from a far country
    there's not much to it

My poems
are simple things
    like reading letters from a far country
    there's no need for tears

My joy and sadness
are even simpler things
    like killing people from a far country
    there's no need for words

[trans. Christopher Drake]

A Visionary   four pieces

A small bird falls from the sky
A field is there
for the single bird shot down when no one was around

A scream comes from a window
The world is there
for the single scream shot to death in a room with no one around

The sky is there for the small bird
                        The small bird falls only from the sky
The window is there for the scream
                        The scream is heard only from the window

I do not know why it is so
I only feel why it is so

For the small bird to fall, there has to be some height
There must be something that is shut tight
for the scream to be heard

Just as there is the small dead bird in the field, death fills my mind
Just as death occupies my mind, no one is at any window in the world

                        *

At first
I was looking out of a small window
at half past four

a dog ran past
a cold fury chasing it

        (Where did the dog come from,
        that skinny dog?

Where did he run off to,
the dog of our times?)
(What darkness is chasing you?
What desire is urging you to run?)

At two o'clock
a pear tree was ripped apart
ants went past dragging a fellow ant's carcass

(So far
what our eyes have seen
always began at its end)
(When we were born
we had long been dead
By the time we hear a scream
only silence remains)

At half past one
a single black bird fell
from an extreme height

(Whose yard is this?
This forsaken yard, so desolate
in the autumn light
Whose is it?)
(You, who are at an extreme height
like a bird looking for prey,
tell me whose yard this is.)

At twelve
with the gaze of one looking into the distance
I looked over the yard

*

The sky is filled with
wreckage adrift in our times
Even a small bird
must pass through our bitter hearts
to return to its dark nest

*

One voice came to an end. At dawn
when I heard it in a bird cage
I did not know
what the voice was after.

One image vanished. At dusk
when I saw it in a rescue boat
I did not know
what gave birth to its shadow.

When that voice forms our sky
after flying out of the bird cage,
when its shadow shapes our horizon
by crushing the rescue boat,

My thirst is at the height of the day

[trans. Takako Lento]

The Thin Line

You are always by yourself
In your eyes where I have never seen tears
there's something like a bitter gleam
I like it

In your sightless imagination
this world is a wilderness for hunting
where you are a hunter in winter
always trying to close in on a single heart

You do not trust words
In your footprints as you have massacred every heart
I see a deep yearning for fear
I cannot stand it

    Along the thin line you walk
    the smell of blood sticks even to the snow
    However far I move away from it
    I can tell

You pull the trigger!
I die inside your words

[trans. Takako Lento]

Standing Coffin

I

Do not touch my corpse
your hands
cannot touch "death"
let my corpse
be among multitudes
let it be beaten by rain

we have no hands
we have no hands to touch death

I know city windows
I know the window where nobody is present
whichever city I went to
you were never in your rooms
marriage, work,
passion, sleep, even death
get chased out of your rooms
to become jobless like you are

we have no jobs
we have no jobs to touch death

I know rain in cities
I know crowds of umbrellas
whichever city I went to
you were never under your roofs
values, beliefs
revolutions, hopes, even lives

get chased out from under your roofs
to become jobless just like you are

we have no jobs
we have no jobs to touch lives

II

Do not lay my corpse on earth
your deaths
cannot rest on earth
rest my corpse
in a standing coffin
and let it stand straight up

on this earth there are no graves for us
on this earth there are no graves to place our corpses

I know death on earth
I know the meaning of death on earth
whichever country I went to
your deaths were never placed in graves
a young woman's corpse flowing down the river,
blood of a small bird shot down, and many slaughtered voices
get chased out of your land
to become exiles just like you are

on this earth there are no countries of ours
on this earth there are no countries that deserve our deaths

I know earthly values
I know lost earthly values
whichever countries I went to

your lives were never filled with something greater
wheat harvested into the future time,
trapped beasts, and young sisters
get chased out of your lives
to become exiles just like you are

     on this earth there are no countries of our own
     on this earth there are no countries deserving our lives

III

Do not burn my corpse with fire
your deaths
cannot be burned with fire
let my corpse
rot
dangling in civilization

we have no fire
we have no fire to burn corpses

I know your civilizations
I know your civilizations without love or death
whichever house I visited
you were never with your families
a drop of a father's tears,
the painful joy of a mother giving birth, even the problems
    of the heart
get chased out of your homes
to become the sick just like you are

     we have no love
     all we have is love of the sick

I know your sick-rooms
I know your dreams that go on from bed to bed
whichever sick room I went to
you were never really asleep
hands hanging off the beds,
eyes wide open to the greater, parched hearts
got kicked out of your sick-rooms
to become the sick just like you are

we have no venom
we have no venom to heal us

[trans. Takako Lento]

Angel

A silence is born
because an angel blocks time
above our heads

Silence while I have my eyes open on a narrow bed
in a third-class sleeper on "Hokuto," departed from Aomori at 20:30—
which angel has blocked my time?

Outside the window in the darkness on the Ishikari Plain
extending to the Kanto Plain
are tens of millions of lonesome lights   Even if I gather them all
I
will not be able to see my angel's face

[trans. Takako Lento]

On My Way Home

I should never have learned words
how much better off I'd be
living in a world where meanings don't matter,
the world with no words

If beautiful words take revenge against you
it's none of my concern
If quiet meanings make you bleed
it also is none of my concern

The tears in your gentle eyes
the pain that drips from your silent tongue—
I'd simply gaze at them and walk away
if our world had no words

In your tears is there as much meaning as in the core of a fruit?
In a drop of your blood is there
a shimmering resonance of the evening glow of this world's sunset?

I should never have learned words
Simply because I know Japanese and bits of a foreign tongue
I stand still inside your tears
I come back alone into your blood

[trans. Takako Lento]

Hoya

Hoya is
in autumn   I am
in pain
beneath the pain
are reasons   attending like roots

A fall wind scrapes the last
heat from anywhere on the Musashino Plain
black, silent Musashino, one point of it
my small house
inside the house
my small room
in the room I light a small lamp
and work toward the pain
until its roots confess
the tall keyaki tree
in the empty back yard

[trans. Christopher Drake]

World Without Words

1

The world without words is the sphere of noon
I am vertical

The world without words is a poem at noonfall
I cannot stay horizontal

2

I must discover the world without words   with words
the globe of noon   noon entirely poem
I am vertical
I cannot stay horizontal

3

Midsummer sun
exactly overhead
I was among
countless rocks
among a corpse
the corpse
of lava
energy lifted straight up
out of a live volcano

Why was every form then
a corpse of energy?
why was every color, every rhythm
a corpse of energy?
a single bird

an eagle
circling slowly
why did it watch
only the forms of energy?
why did it not judge
each color and rhythm?

Rock corpses
I drank some milk
bit into my bread like a grenade thrower

4

The incandescent flow itself
resisting fluidity, the frozen flame
unfueled by love or fear
forms of energy hugely dead

5

The bird's eyes are evil itself
they watch without judging
the bird's tongue is evil itself
it swallows without judging

6

Sharply split tongue of a starred dove
flicking spear of a great spotted woodpecker
sculpting-knife tongue of a woodcock
soft cutter in the mouth of a golden thrush
it watches without judging
it swallows without judging

I went down a path
cold as Pluto
eight miles to the hut
down the path of death and sex
enormous out-tide falling endlessly

I am a grenade thrower
I am a shipwrecked sailor
I am a bird's eyes
I am an owl's tongue

I watch with blind eyes
I open my blind eyes and fall
my tongue hangs out and I unbark trees
my tongue's not for licking love and justice
its jagged barbs won't heal fear and hunger

The path of death and sex
path of small animals and insects
a band of bees bends and breaks away
thousands of needles lying in ambush
path without judgments and counter-judgments
without the meaning of meaning
without judgments of judgments
path without empty structures, minor desires
without metaphors, symbols, all imagination
only destruction and reproduction
only reconstruction, pieces
fragments and fragments of fragments

splinters and splinters of splinters
designs woven within always larger designs
path of similes freezing in June
air sacs extending from scarlet lungs
birds fly
ice-cold sacs filling bones with air
birds fly within birds

10

The bird's eyes are evil itself
the bird's tongue is evil itself
it destroys but does not build
it recreates but does not create
it is a fragment   fragment within a fragment
it has air sacs but no empty mind
its eyes and tongue are evil itself
but it is not evil

burn, bird
burn, birds, all birds
burn, birds, animals, all animals
burn, death and sex
burn, path of death and sex
burn

11

Midsummer cold as Pluto
path frozen hard as Pluto
down the path of death and sex
running
floating
flying
I am a grenade thrower

and I am the enemy
I am a sailor wrecked on the rocks
and I am the outrushing tide
I am a bird
and I am its blind hunter
I am the hunter
I am the enemy
enemy completely without fear

12

At sunset
I'll have reached the hut
the low scrub will be forest
the lava flow, the sun, the falling tide
will be intercepted by my tiny dream

the water will taste bitter
I'll drink a glass slowly, as if it were poison
I'll close my eyes and open them again
I'll cut my whisky with water

13

I won't go back to the hut
words can't be cut
with meaning

[trans. Christopher Drake]

Water

Any death is merely a pause
Poetry is the renunciation of "completion"

I had a drink of water
at the foot of Mount Ooyama in Kanagawa

It had scent and taste
I could even hear its sound

Poetry is in essence a fixed form
Anyone's life has alliteration and rhyme

[trans. Takako Lento]

Dead Leaves

And
they died without shedding green
blood

Before returning to earth
they turn into
the color of the earth
the color of
Silence that died its death

Why is everything
so lucid?
we walked on and on
along the border of day and night
among dead leaves

Those under fixed
stars
do not look back

[trans. Takako Lento]

The Man with a Green Face

It was a beautiful morning
shoulder to shoulder
we watched the squadron sail out of sight
to the very end we believed
that a huge silence commanded
the sea of freedom and necessity
and that only illusions were real

Of course the squadron never returned
to any port   to any homeland
of course reality was an illusion
shoulder to shoulder
we scanned every mile of horizon
but necessity and freedom
were always within history—
only the man with a green face
tries to break out of history—
we let go of each other's shoulders
the beautiful morning shatters
between our dangling arms

We need more cunning to hunger harder
more imagination to end our dreaming
we have to leave "we" behind
you won't find the man with a green face
in a group or a crowd
and if you say that only evil exists
then history will whisper back:
all great things are evil

[trans. Christopher Drake]

Perhaps a Great Poem

A poem rests, barely, on a single line
a kind of balance of terror
humans must hold out their arms
and endure this balance—
a moment's dizziness
will tilt your whole life

Perhaps a great poem
travels faster than the speed of light
forcing humans
to invade the present from the future
and the past from the present—
a dead man steps out of the ground,
returns to the hands of those who buried him,
then, moving backwards, continues on
to the flesh-colored dark that bore him,
the original birthing spring;
love moves from destruction toward completion
all things begin in their ending:
the permanent revolution
the withered-away state
a single poem

Perhaps a great poem is
in November light—
the light that pierces every object
making humans close their eyes,
stretch out their arms, stand precisely there

[trans. Christopher Drake]

The House of Man

I may be back late
that's what I said when I left my house
my house is made of words
in my old closet is a glacier
in my bathroom is a horizon I have yet to see
desert and time come out of my phone
bread, salt and water on the dining table
a woman lives in the water
a hyacinth is blooming out of the woman's eyeball
the woman is also a metaphor herself
she changes the way words do
because she is as amorphous as a cat
I have no way of knowing even her name

I may be back late
not that I have a business meeting or a reunion
I take an ice train
walk down fluorescent colored underground paths
cross the shadow square and
get into a mollusk elevator
in the train I see violet tongues, gray lips
on the underground path I find rainbow-colored throats, green lungs
in the square I find frothing language, information from the
     language, information from the information
adjectives: every possible empty adjective
adverbs: coarse and unsightly adverbs
nouns: boring boring nouns are in abundance but
there are no verbs whichever way I turn
all I want is verbs

I am sick and tired of a society made solely of future and past tenses
what I want is the present tense

when you open a door, it doesn't mean you find a room behind it
when there is a window, you can't say there's an indoor space beyond it
you can't say there's space for people to live and die

so far
I've opened countless doors
have closed them and
have gotten out
to enter through another door
what marvelous new world could be behind that door?
what can you hear? from the other side of paradise
dripping water
the beating wings of a bird
a rising tide breaking against boulders at a headland
the breathing of humans and beasts
the smell of blood

come to think of it
I forgot the smell of blood
for quite a long time
where silence converges into one scream
the tip of a needle

a surgeon slowly approaches putting on rubber gloves
I open my eyes, and close them
something falls into the depths of my eyes
holding both arms open like wings
hair standing on end
it keeps falling through the momentary fissure of light connecting
        darkness to darkness

I stand up slowly from a table in a bar
my idea of going home is not based on political belief or religious
        creed

I just want to see with my own eyes
the collapse of the house of man
the deconstruction of my language

of course my house is not made of your words
my house is made of my words

[trans. Takako Lento]

Gods of Poetry

Mokichi's gods of poetry
were the Asakusa Kannon and broiled eels

Because he walled his poems with solid form
he only had to go to the temple's Thunder Gate

My nervous gods of poetry
pacing, pacing, have no fire insurance

Small houses
large silences

[trans. Christopher Drake]

Every Morning after Killing Thousands of Angels

1

I read a boy's poem called
"Every Morning after Killing Thousands of Angels"
I forget the poem, but the title won't leave me
I drink some coffee
read a paper read by millions
all the misery
all the destruction in the world
herded into headlines and catch phrases
the only part I trust
is the financial page
a completely blank space governed
by the mechanics of capital and pure speculation

2

That boy's mornings
and my mornings—
how are they different?

3

But the boy can see the angels' faces

4

What do you do
after you kill them?

I go out walking

Where?

To a river with a very big bridge over it

Every morning?

Every morning
while my hands are still bloody

5

I can't kill thousands of angels
so I walk a dry path to the beach
the hot sky's still filled
with sweating typhoon clouds
the sea's a later color
fall is not summer at the horizon
narrow streams run through
spaces silted with darkness
weak-looking capillaries float on my thin hands:
no place to anchor a big bridge

6

Noon at this end of the bridge
everything shines
shirt buttons
decayed tooth
an air rifle
broken sunglass lens
pink shells
smell of seaweed
river water mixing with the sea

sand
and
as far
as my footprints

7

It's my turn now
I'll tell you about the world
at the far end of the bridge
the shadow world
things and concepts totally shadow
shadows feeding on shadows
spreading, radiating like cancer cells
decomposing organs of drowned bodies
green thought swelling and distending
medieval markets surging with merchants and prostitutes and monks
cats, sheep, hogs, horses, cows
every kind of meat on the butcher shop hooks
but no blood anywhere

8

So I can't see the bridge
unless I kill thousands of angels?

9

You know what sight excites me most sexually?
the bridge has disappeared
a riderless black horse
crosses the world of light
slowly, toward the shadow world
but exhausted, it falls

crying animals tears but not rotting
gleaming directly to bone
pure white bone
and then to earth
and then
dawn comes
I've got to go out and live
after killing
killing thousands of angels

[trans. Christopher Drake]

Green Conceptual Body

Dogs run inside dogs
cats sleep inside cats
birds fly inside birds nailed to the sky
fish swim panting in the water across deserts inside fish

But people can't run inside inner people
so they run inside conceptual bodies
they can't sleep free-form cat sleep
so they watch insomniac dreams
they can't swim like fish
so they labor to float concepts
and they can't fly like birds
so they put wings on concepts
to feel the pleasure of crashing

Sometimes people
are inside rooms
but they never live
inside people (inside bodies)
people sleep inside different concepts,
choose vegetables over meat,
boil, fry, make eating a chore;
concepts peer into the blood,
make people need forks and chopsticks
people even need shovels to bury corpses
stopping to lick ice cream as they work

People go out walking
on nice days in early summer
leaving the people inside themselves in their rooms;
these shut-in bodies measure their blood pressure and spoon out honey
and lead thoughts across their voices;
what does the spirit, shut in, do?
what went out walking

weren't bodies, weren't spirit
were conceptual bodies with legs
they built the vertical nightmare of medieval Gothic
the ascending nightmare knotting heaven and earth
invisible ropes
hierarchical classes
wings for angels
ivory horns for devils
the materials had to be combustible
the dream irreversible

I walk a small path through the field
and come out by the Tama River
on the other side two men tend fishing lines
no conceptual bodies: people
drowsy, I lie down in the grass—that instant
the vertical axis swings, the horizontal
pushes through my conceptual body
the Gothic collapses
voluptuous curves and colors spurt out
the smell of water comes this far

Sun directly overhead
objects but no shadows
my conceptual body turns cat-indeterminate
its footsteps
utterly soundless

Leaving one dream to enter another,
you can hardly call that waking;
I have no Globe to world
my thoughts to actors on the stage—
I'd rather look, for a split second,
at the most modern nightmare, nuclear war
but the moment I saw it
because I had come to the edge of the field
they would be watching me: eyes in

angelic missiles and beautiful hydrogen bombs;
I'm not a passerby, not a spectator
I myself am the nightmare

All I still want
is, on the tongues of gravediggers,
the taste of ice cream.

[trans. Christopher Drake]

The Day the Mercury Sank

A deer at bay will fall from the cliff,
but for a human being to fall,
there has to be a poem.

The day the mercury sank,
I was visiting a cheap apartment
in the East Village in New York.

Downstairs was a printer and a law office.
The poet's room was on the second floor,
with just a typewriter and scattered sheets of music.

Of course, there's nothing novel about a poet's workroom.
In a painter or sculptor's atelier,
there is a faint scent of

the secrets of creation and destruction of form.
What we had here was strong coffee, a dry martini, and a pack of
        Lucky Strike.
I couldn't quite keep up with poet's English,

so I just looked at the wall. A portrait of E. M. Forster
and a watercolor of an Austrian mountain villa:
enough to bring this poet's secret to light.
The "individual" who acknowledged himself heir to Victorian culture,
        Austrian forest,
and New York backstreets.

> *Japan, I was there in 1938. It was just for an hour at Haneda.*
> *We went right to wartime China,*
> *Isherwood and I.*

The day the mercury sank,
I was in "In Time of War."
The poet's great hand shook mine in farewell.

[trans. Marianne Tarcov]

Lieberman Goes Home

Rainy day man, Lieberman, is going home
to the wide open cornfields of the American Midwest.
"From the pier in Yokohama
oh, all aboard . . ."
With his two daughters and one son tucked under his arms
and the support of his polar bear of a wife,
he's going back to the University of Illinois.
If you don't get back soon,
your professorial position's going to get stolen
by some women's lib professor. It doesn't rain very much in Illinois,
so get as wet as you can in the rainy season of Japan.
Oh! Get those big blue eyes wet:
our manic-depressive Lieberman is going home.
So we're having a goodbye party.
Kamakura is just about starting the rainy season,
and while the pond may not be quite as big as Lake Michigan, it is
    infested with wobbling mosquito larvae.
So up I wobble to my feet,
whisky tipsy,
and make a speech. Niikura translates.
When our rainy day man first got to Kamakura,
Niikura did the talking,
from negotiations for renting a place to repairing the gas in the
    bath, converting every last dollar into yen.
When the yen was revaluated, the dollar dropped. The rainy day
    man dropped to his knees and wept.
Our rainy day man is a poet, so he wrote a poem for *The New
    Yorker*: "The Dollar's Lament."
He pocketed the contributor's fee, so here we are in this fine
    restaurant.

Lieberman is a big fan of fresh yellowtail sushi chock-full of
    Japanese toxic chemicals.

So the sushi chef says, *What do you do, sir, if I may ask?*
The rainy day man, his nose twitching with hungry anticipation,
    says in his mild Japanese,
I'm a Poe yet.
What! Poe yet?
No, poet!
Oh. You're a poet.
Here I am, all a-wobble, trying to give my speech. So here's the
    speech:
So long as you're in Japan,
you're a university professor, got it?
Poets are bums.
This isn't the Midwest, where the sun sets
in shimmering flame among the cornfields.
Genuine poets are brawny farmers. But in Japan we've got a bunch of
petty progressive peasants. When it comes to America, all they can do
is keep talking about the Viet Nam War and racism . . .
I'm so drunk, I don't know what I'm talking about.
The interpreter is so drunk, he doesn't know what he's talking
    about either.
Only our rainy day man is staring into space, staring. Into space.
Well, so long! Bon voyage!
Forget about Japan!
See you later, hippo hipster! *Arigato*, alligator!

[trans. Marianne Tarcov]

My Imperialism

Resting in bed
since Pentecost Monday
I bless myself
since I'm not a Christian

Yet my ears still wander the sky
my eyes keep hunting for underground water
and my hands hold a small book
describing the grotesqueness of modern white society
when looked down at from the nonwhite world
in my fingers there's a thin cigarette—
I wish it were hallucinogenic
though I'm tired of indiscriminate ecstasy

Through a window in the northern hemisphere
the light moves slowly past morning to afternoon
before I can place the red flare, it's gone:
darkness

Yes, my acupuncturist came on Pentecost Monday morning
a graduate student in Marxist economics, he says he changed
to medicine to help humanity, the animal of animals, drag itself
    peacefully to its deathbeds
forty years of Scotch whisky's roasted my liver and put me
into the hands of a Marxist economist
I want to ask him about *Imperialism, A Study*—
what Hobson saw in South Africa at the end of the nineteenth century
may yet push me out of bed
even if you wanted to praise imperialism

there aren't enough kings and natives left
the overproduced slaves had to become white

Only the nails grow
the nails of the dead grow too
so, like cats, we must constantly
sharpen ours to stay alive
Only The Nails Grow—not a bad epitaph
when K died his wife buried him in Fuji Cemetery
and had To One Woman carved on his gravestone
true, it was the title of one of his books
but the way she tried to have him only
to herself almost made me cry
even N, who founded the modernist magazine *Luna*
while Japan prepared to invade China
got sentimental after he went on his pension;
F, depressed
S, manic, builds house after house
A has abdominal imperialism: his stomach's colonized his legs
M's deaf, he can endure the loudest sounds;
some people have only their shadows grow
others become smaller than they really are
our old manifesto had it wrong: we only looked upward
if we'd really wanted to write poems
we should have crawled on the ground on all fours—
when William Irish, who wrote *The Phantom Lady*, died
the only mourners were stock brokers
Mozart's wife was not at his funeral

My feet grow warmer as I read
Kotoku Shusui's *Imperialism, Monster of the Twentieth Century*, written
     back in 1901
when he was young N wrote "I say strange things"
was it the monster that pumped tears from his older eyes?

Poems are commodities without exchange value
but we're forced to invade new territory
by crises of poetic overproduction

We must enslave the natives with our poems
all the ignorant savages under sixty
plagued by a surplus of clothes and food—
when you're past sixty
you're neither a commodity
nor human

[trans. Christopher Drake]

Alluring Precipice

"Wherever you are, an alluring precipice is within sight"
a French philosopher theorized
but I see
no precipice at all
The horizon over the sea, the horizon over the land,
the moon rising in the East with the sun setting in the West on the
    Nepali grasslands
whose peaceful scenery took my heart away, yet
none of them will become the "alluring precipice"
perhaps because my eyes have yet to become naked
I must have walked this earth by sight alone for over seventy years
first I must explore the mysteries of warmth
must know the gradual decomposition of flesh, that perishable
    substance

That is the moment Love is born
those who live by sight alone cannot experience Love
a life form is *stuff*
the instincts of a life form are also *stuff*
yet
when sight morphs into naked eyes
a thing will be reborn as a heart
even if you travel to the ends of the earth
you'll see only *stuff* if you only have sight

Even if ten million, ten billion life forms vanish in a flash
in the moment naked eyes cause
a nucleo-fusion of a thing and a heart
this world has something that will not disappear

[trans. Takako Lento]

Images

Tamura as a child, circa 1926-7.

Tamura in his naval uniform in 1943 (20 years old).

Tamura (center) in 1956, 33 years old, at the publication party for
Four Thousand Days and Nights, with fellow *Arechi* poets Ayukawa
Nobuo (left) and Yoshimoto Takaaki (right).

First postwar volume of *Arechi* (*Wasteland*), published in September 1947.

Tamura at his desk.

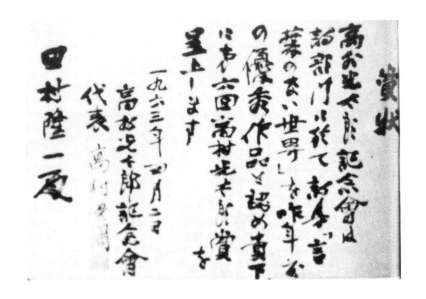

The 6th Takamura Kotaro Award, 1963:

Award

Poetry Division of Takamura Kotaro Memorial Conference recognizes
World Without Words *as the best work produced during the past year
and awards the sixth Takamura Kotaro Award.*

April 2, 1963

to Tamura Ryuichi

Tamura with whisky.

Tamura in his garden.

Essays

Introduction to *Dead Languages*

Christopher Drake

In February, 1942, Tamura Ryuichi wrote that the most pow-
erful modern Japanese poem was this announcement from the
Japanese high command on December 8th, 1941 (December 7th
in the Western hemisphere): "Before dawn this morning, the 8th,
the Imperial Army and Navy entered a condition of combat with
American and British forces in the Western Pacific." No other mod-
ern Japanese poem, Tamura said, had with so few words, in fact
only a single line, made so many people shudder so deeply.

This was Tamura's answer to an examination question given by
modernist poet and teacher Hagiwara Sakutaro. He was not praising
the military, the emperor, or the attack on Pearl Harbor; rather he
was beginning to write his own history of modern Japanese poetry,
a history that he has still not finished and one that has claimed many
of his best poems, a history that looks always for a "next line," a
line beyond and behind every uttered or written line. For Tamura
the next line to the December 8th declaration, and the only line so
far to surpass it, was the emperor's terse radio broadcast of August
15th, 1945, announcing Japan's surrender. This line negated, de-

stroyed the first; for a few immense seconds, perhaps even minutes, the Japanese language had no shadows.

Destruction and creation, light and shadow, have collided and coincided almost as intensely in Tamura's own life. An offspring of destruction, he is one of its most relentless interrogators. His life parallels almost exactly one of the most deadly periods in Japanese history, and his poems continue to uncover deeper levels of damage as they probe the invisible fault lines that cross and recross contemporary Japanese culture.

Tamura's birth on March 18th, 1923, in the Tokyo suburb of Otsuka preceded by less than six months the great Kanto earthquake that devastated much of Tokyo and Yokohama [. . .], a disaster that proved to be one of the main watersheds in Japan's turn toward militarism. Democracy suffered as police-inspired rightwing vigilance committees massacred more than 6,000 labor organizers and Korean migrant workers during the confusion. And the economy suffered: earthquake damage played a major role in the bank crisis of 1927, which in turn contributed to monopoly control of finance and increased militarization of production, especially after Japan invaded China in 1931 (when Tamura was eight) and attacked the United States and Britain (when Tamura was eighteen).

The great earthquake also changed literary history. The poet Kaneko Mitsuharu, seeing the fragility of the European-oriented Tokyo elite writer cliques, set out on the first of his vagabond journeys to China and southeast Asia—voyages that resulted in the first modern Japanese poetry that was based neither on European nor on nationalistic Japanese models.

As a child Tamura was only indirectly aware of these large events. The earthquake, ironically, spared Otsuka, and the area quickly became a major gathering place for refugees, including many from Tokyo's traditional entertainment and brothel districts. Tamura grew up in the back room of a restaurant owned by his grandfather and run by his parents, who had become suddenly prosperous catering to this new population. More than six hundred geishas and a large number of other entertainers and performing artists worked in Otsuka then, and in the restaurant and the "trysting houses" nearby, Tamura watched and listened as they played shamisen, danced, and sang traditional songs night after night. Much of his education was left to his grandparents, who remembered the words and tales of premodern Tokyo (Edo) and spoke in rhythms from an older, more humorous, and more sensual age that had already died in the memories of most people during Japan's forced march toward westernization after 1868. Tamura was especially fond of his raconteur grandfather, whose hobby was holding huge, days-long parties with geishas and Sumo wrestlers, and who loved to take his grandson along to see Kabuki plays at the Ichimuraza theater and to visit hot springs and entertainment spots all over the country during school vacations. The view from Tamura's bedroom window also was educational: beyond a semitransparent hanging screen stood the examining table of the local gynecologist.

When he wasn't with his grandfather, Tamura spent most of his time surrounded by working women performing public roles in a tightly-organized community. "Most of the students at my grade school," Tamura later wrote, "had some connection with the 'gay quarters' (*karyukai*, the World of Blossoms and Willows). Not many came from 'decent' families. The girls were either daughters of geishas or students learning the geisha arts. By the time I entered college almost all of them had become full-fledged geisha artists. (Even now there are some tryst-house managers and aging geishas who call me 'Little Ryu.') In my experience, at least, no one in the gay quarters really belongs to a family. It's a self-enclosed world all to itself where you're constantly running into people you've never seen before, where morning and evening are reversed, and where people use secret languages and metaphors."

Living in this anti-world governed largely by women, seeing the women in their off hours and without makeup, Tamura was never tempted by the romantic adoration of "ideal" women found in much early modern Japanese poetry. Many of the cooks, waitresses, geishas, and prostitutes came from starving farm families in the north and spoke in rough, earthy accents; they appeared to Tamura as anything but beautiful innocents. Although Tamura has written some of the most erotic postwar Japanese poems [. . .] his images avoid a purely esthetic definition of women. From the beginning Tamura has regarded erotic energy as the source rather than the subject of poetry.

Tamura's early world and the self he developed within it became the source of acute shame and suffering after he entered middle school. The school was located beyond the borders of the Otsuka gay quarters, and most of its students were from families working at "straight" professions. Tamura felt humiliated even by the sound of the word "restaurant" as it was pronounced by outsiders, and, soon, by himself. The first syllable of *ryoriya*, "restaurant," partially overlaps the first syllable of Tamura's first name, Ryuichi. "Whenever," he later wrote," I told anyone that my parents ran a restaurant, they would all, without exception, look at me strangely. It was exactly the same expression people get when they open the door of a stall in a public lavatory and find somebody squatting inside."

Tamura first came across written poetry in 1935, at a commercial high school in rebuilt downtown Tokyo, an hour and a half by train and streetcar from his home in Otsuka. This was also Tamura's first exposure to the outside world. He still remembers passing the Bank of Japan on the snowy morning of February 26th, 1936, finding it guarded by grimfaced soldiers, and learning later that an ultranationalistic young officers' mutiny had virtually ended civilian control of the military.

At school Tamura hated business classes but liked English (his advanced text was Malthus' *An Essay on the Principle of Population*) and the Chinese classics. He was also exposed to traditional Japanese No drama and tanka poetry.

"Getting away from Otsuka," Tamura recalls, "was a real liberation, an escape from all the falseness of a town trying to keep alive an artificial culture that it got secondhand from old Edo. Otsuka was like one of those American towns on the Mississippi that pretend to be living in the 19th century and end up living nowhere."

Another of Tamura's several selves, however, one that was never fully destroyed by his renunciation of his birthplace and that never fully consented to calling the gay quarters "bad" or "old-fashioned," seems to have had a voice in the writing of Tamura's first poem. That poem was published in a small mimeographed magazine called *Elm* (*Erumu*) put out at the high school with his only Otsuka classmate, the son of a popular geisha who had several poets among her customers. No copies of the magazine remain, but Tamura still remembers the first line of his first poem, a line he and his friend found as funny as it was frightening: *yurei no kasso . . .*, "The gliding of ghosts . . ." Again uncannily, the two syllables of "ghost" (*yurei*) reversed become a sounds (*reiyu*) echoing Tamura's own first name. These half-humorous, half-otherworldly spirits have never ceased circling Tamura, turning his most stubbornly straight lines into spirals and patiently waiting for him to look down and see his own feet turning.

In high school Tamura met Kitamura Taro (who was four months older) and Yoshimoto Takaaki (who was a year and a half younger), both of whom would later, like Tamura, contribute to the postwar Wasteland group publications. Kitamura introduced Tamura to several small modernist magazines during 1939, including *Le Bal* and *Shinryodo*. *Le Bal* (*The Ball*) was edited by Nakagiri Masao, Ayukawa Nobuo, and other future Wasteland members, and dedicated, as its name suggests, to poetry as purely mental play. *Shinryodo* was a Japanese translation of *New Country*, the 1933 British anthology whose milder poems included Auden's "A Communist to Others." *Shinryodo*, however, devoted itself to abstract modernism and had little of *New Country*'s ethical urgency or political advocacy. Yet Tamura never forgot the poems of Auden, Spender, Day Lewis and the rest, and after the experience of World War Two they took on a new life for him.

In the meantime, Japan launched a full-scale invasion of China in 1937 and at home instigated a period of thought control and patriotic hysteria. Poets were pulled into the vortex. Even Hagiwara Sakutaro (mentioned above), the first major modern free verse poet and an outspoken supporter of Western thought and poetry, suddenly published in 1937 a book, *Coming Full Circle*, in which he claimed to have realized that Western civilization was no more substantial than the mythical seabottom palace of the Dragon King in an ancient Japanese myth.

In this unreal atmosphere Ayukawa translated *The Waste Land* in 1940, and with friends put out a small magazine, *Wasteland*, which took from Eliot's poem a central image but not all its metaphysics. This was Tamura's first exposure to Eliot. Shortly afterward *Wasteland* magazine was suppressed (its title was declared "dangerously negative"), and *Shinryodo*, whose September 1939 issue had been suppressed for an extremely abstract reference to the Japanese invasion of China, was forced to cease publication in 1941. The friends scattered, some forever.

To avoid the draft, Tamura entered Meiji University in the spring of 1941. There he spent most of his time reading Thomas Mann and Kabuki plays and memorizing traditional Japanese Rakugo comic stories. When he heard the December 8th radio broadcast declaring war on the U.S. and Britain, his first impulse was to go to Ginza to see a foreign film, his last chance he guessed rightly, to see one for a long time. At this time Takamura Kotaro, one of the greatest prewar free verse poets, was writing lines like "Remember December 8th / It cut world history in two!" and the renowned modern tanka poet Saito Mokichi (addressed in Tamura's poem "Gods of Poetry") was writing "When I hear / that war / has started / I hear the roar / of victory itself."

Tamura's second impulse, after hearing these and other patriotic outbursts by formerly independent and individualistic poets and writers, was to assert that the greatest modern poem was the Japanese high command's announcement of war. And while many poets continued to think they could write poems greater than that irreducible, absolute poem of the modern Japanese state, Tamura kept silent throughout the war.

In October 1943 his student draft-deferment ended and Tamura had to make another hard choice. After hearing from Ayukawa about the horrors of army life, Tamura, pockets stuffed with Stendhal, Rimbaud, and Nagai Kafu's *Strange Tale from East of the Sumida River*, joined the navy. In February 1944 he failed the naval pilot's examination (he was too tall to fit easily into the tiny cockpit of a Zero fighter) and was sent for basic training to

Kagoshima, in southern Kyushu. In September he was transferred north to Shiga Prefecture on Honshu, and in July 1945 to artillery duty on the shore of Wakasa Bay, northwest of Kyoto, where a U.S. or Russian invasion was expected. The invasion never came. Tamura, unlike many of his friends in Kagoshima who were ordered to kill themselves as kamikaze pilots, survived; but he has never gotten over the experience of being certain he would die, and he has never stepped out of earshot of the voices of those who did die.

The setting for Tamura's shore duty in the navy was as irretrievably incongruous as a surrealist poem. He was stationed in a 14th-century Zen temple whose main image, ironically, was a sculptured shamanic maternity deity believed to bring easy childbirth. The temple looked out over some of the bluest water in Japan, so blue that its very color seemed to forbid the intrusion of ships. Yet when Tamura and the others stripped down to loincloths and dove in they could never be sure of swimming back to shore alive.

At war's end, a whole generation of Japanese writers had been sent off to war and forced to look at more than literature. More than 2.5 million Japanese had died; many more were injured; still more were in a state of psychological shock and disbelief at the sudden collapse of a universe of values they had thought absolute. A number of poets went into self-imposed (though temporary) exile in remote regions of the country, and even the gentle, softly mystical poet Shaku Choku (Orikuchi Shinobu) was so shaken he spent forty days wandering in the mountains. When Tamura and his friends regathered in the remains of Tokyo, however, they were looking toward the future, searching for intense fragments of meaning that would somehow make more apparent the deeper deceptions and counterfeit images underlying and making possible modern Japanese culture as a whole. Tokyo—including Otsuka—had been reduced to ashes, but bombers had been helpless to touch the invisible wreckage still filling the Japanese sky (consider Tamura's poem "A Visionary").

The friends straggled home at different times. Makino Kyotaro and Morikawa Nobuyoshi had been killed, Ayukawa Nobuo and

Kihara Koichi had been hospitalized, Nakagiri Masao and Miyoshi Toyoichiro had tuberculosis, and Tamura was shaking his head wondering how and why he was still alive. Kitamura Taro and Kuroda Saburo returned relatively sound physically, although Kuroda seems to have left much of his heart with the Indonesian independence forces by whom he was arrested and with whom he stayed for almost a year after the surrender.

Tamura spent three weeks with a friend in Kyoto and then returned to Tokyo in September. His family's house had been completely burned, so he slept on a number of people's floors for the next few months. In 1946 he got a job editing children's picture books, and soon he was using the second floor of the company as the meeting place for the Wasteland group. The revived *Wasteland* magazine, filled with their poems and essays, ran for six issues from September 1947 to June 1948. Then the group published a book, *Wasteland Poems 1951*, which was followed by similar anthologies until 1958 (these influential anthologies continue to be reprinted). Two special collections and a *Wasteland Poem Anthology* were also published. *Wasteland* was always more a temporary junction of individualists, a rambling, ambulatory angle of intersection, than a structured group. "Our favorite activity after criticizing each other's poems," Kitamura Taro says, "was criticizing each other's personalities. Nobody could afford to act pompous or literary when we got together." He adds, "We did have fun together sometimes too. I remember that we even wrote haiku together. Tamura's haiku were hilarious, the most humorous of all. But I doubt if any of them remain, anywhere." The group's will to doubt every thing and every value, to reduce every aspect and artifact of modern civilization to ash so it could be recreated, remained incandescent until about 1954, when, amazingly, it began to give prizes and hunt for new "members." "Actually," Kitamura says, "we didn't plan to stay together that long. By then there were younger poets like Ooka Makoto and Tanikawa Shuntaro who also knew how to put mind and world and poem together, so we knew we were history."

Tamura's first book, *Four Thousand Days and Nights*, appeared in 1956. Tamura is both the most and least typical Wasteland poet.

Like the others, he tried to go beyond prewar modernism, which had imported only the abstract and esthetic elements of dada, surrealism, and the rest, and ignored their bursts of meaning and their critical edge (several leading Japanese surrealists and so-called proletarian poets ended up writing nationalistic poems during World War Two). And, also like the others, Tamura worked toward a critique of world culture through the discovery of universal images. "We weren't nihilists," he says. "We were glad to be the living dead with nothing to lose. We wanted to question the basic principles behind an industrial society based on the illusion of the isolated individual and the deification of economic growth based on war and imperialism. I tried to make my poems into holes or windows, to catch sight of the invisible spiritual waste as well as the obvious material destruction."

After 1945, when most people assumed the war had ended, Tamura discovered ways to bypass the old anti-philosophical Japanese lyric mode. He moved freely, writing public poetry about the continuing war between the myth of Japanese postwar progress and democratization and the tiny, almost inaudible voices of those—including the souls of the war dead—who actually looked and listened.

Tamura had been almost uniquely successful in creating fictional speakers in his poems and in breaking away from the confessional monolog voice-of-authority that so obsessed prewar Japanese poets and novelists. In fact, Tamura considers the greatest work of prewar modern Japanese literature (with the possible exception of Kaneko Mitsuhara's *Sharks* poems) to be the diary of the prose fictionalist Nagai Kafu because Kafu's written "I" is part of the public, material world, wryly distanced from his self-conscious confessional ego. This non-subjective "I" has little stake in proving the purity of its privacy; it is a self that always includes at least one non-self. Similarly, Tamura has written that his own prose poem "Etching" is the "basic form" of all his later poems because it includes both a "he" and an "I" who manage to limit each other: in their violent collision comes a moment of achieved honesty. The single-voiced poet thinks he or she is a unique center of meaning and that personal wounds are as absolute and beautiful as flowers. The lonely, apparently confessional "I" appears to Tamura as an emperor in disguise.

"The emperor," says Tamura speaking of another prose poem, "is Napoleon, is Hirohito, is me." By extension, war can be seen as the ultimate lyric poem, the expression by a private group or state of the absolute primacy of its own "my feeling." Through the lyric a poet can reduce him- or herself to an "I"; through war a nation can act as though it were a single subject.

Tamura has developed many anti-lyric strategies, but his poems also depend for much of their power on an intuitive grasp of folk rhythms, on ancient traditions of self-parody, and on the pre-Buddhist Japanese identification of death with sensuality and rebirth. "The Sunken Cathedral,"[1] whose title comes from Debussy, is a good example of Tamura's unconscious yet firm grasp of the Japanese oral song tradition of statement modified by counterstatement. In this prose poem an impressionistic Europe-like dream-world described by a melancholy "I" is shattered by the young man in the second fragment whose statement is both moving and comic. The differing, confrontational voices in "Standing Coffin" and "Three Voices"[2] present not only the moanings of those trapped in mass society but also echo old Japanese elegiac songs and mythic texts in their almost religious intensity. One of Tamura's favorite mirrors, the diving bird, also recalls images from an archaic age in which the soul was considered to be an ellipsis of altitude.

In *World Without Words* (1962) and subsequent works, Tamura moves out into the material world of wild birds and animals and even minerals. After living for about three years near the foot of Mt. Asama, one of Japan's largest active volcanoes—one located on the seam of two colliding continental plates that will, in the near geological future, halve Honshu and spatter apart the Japanese islands—Tamura comes upon traces of another of his selves. Track-

---

[1] "The Sunken Cathedral" isn't included in the folio of Tamura's poems, but can be read on page 81 at the beginning of Ooka Makoto's essay, translated by Takako Lento.
[2] Not included in this volume.

ing footprints in the snow he finds himself on a long lava flow left by the great eruption of 1783; he feels a coffin rise up his throat, through his head, and toward the noon sun dead above him. 1783 was a time when the conjunction of samurai statecraft, Confucian bureaucracy, and artistic estheticism, all of which made possible the invention of the Meiji absolutist state after 1868, was solidifying into its decisive form. In the vast lava flow that spreads out beneath him Tamura finds a visible substance that has become almost as hard and fixed as Japanese culture has become in the last several centuries. But at last he has found evidence of an unredeemably physical poem, a poem more objective than the emperor's surrender broadcast of August 1945. Truths were hidden all too quickly in 1945 behind imported slogans claiming "freedom of the press" and "democracy," but the witness of the lava will not move. Its immobility is also its strength. It is a fossilized shadow that points back through time to the sun.

After leaving the mountain Tamura realizes that his task as a poet is to discover smoke and steam coming from the hard crust of the Japanese language, to find cracks and gaps and sinkholes that do not exclude eruptions. The point at which invisible planets of language orbit with uncountable rapidity through the feverish, decaying bodies of soft human beings is one such volcano. In approaching the body as a sun at midnight, Tamura must abandon modernism's anatomical esthetics, which seek to convert the body into lyric, personal space. The warm, yet delicately decomposing body is for Tamura the "human house," and in his later poems he seeks—even crawling on his stomach—to hold his house above the deepest rifts in his language, even when these lines turn out to be open graves.

The syntactically integrated, almost Gothic human subject of the Western tradition continues to gain prestige and legitimacy in Japan. Yet Tamura suggests that the imperatives of this heroically abrupt ego are perhaps most elegantly expressed by the hydrogen bomb, a form of confession leaving no space for difference or dissent. Neither, of course, does Tamura look nostalgically toward feudal values and images. In his most recent poems he describes

contemporary Japan as a slave society in which people are trans-
formed into inflections of the objects they have been taught to
need and identify with. Tokyo has become a modern Pompeii, its
self-enclosed human houses standardized and prefabricated under
the pressure of endless tons of cindered language. Without sug-
gesting ultimate solutions, Tamura asserts once more in "My Im-
perialism" the primacy of public, critical poetry in spite of the
increasingly subjective demands of his aging body—and in spite of
the fact that most of the other former Wasteland poets who still
survive have subsided into the slave dialect of private sentiment.
Finally, in "The Other World," Tamura seems to have found a rift
line that defies geometry but that moves as surely as a wrinkle
through skin toward the once-far world of his own near dead. He
turns and there, once more, is his "bad," erotic grandfather who
lived to love so many women and who was born in the very year
Japan set out to try to leave its Other World and sleep with the West.

(1984, *Tamura Ryuichi: Dead Languages*)

CHRISTOPHER DRAKE first met Tamura Ryuichi when Tamura gave a read-
ing at Harvard in 1971, and he was able to interview Tamura several times
in Japan while preparing *Dead Languages* for publication. Drake taught com-
parative literature at Atomi University in Tokyo for three decades and has
published many articles about, and translations of, contemporary Japanese
poetry, haikai and renga linked verse, and Ryukyuan shamanic songs. He
is presently working on an annotated translation of Ihara Saikaku's famous
haibun novel *Life of a Sensuous Man* (1682) as well a translation of Saikaku's
thousand-link haikai requiem for his wife after she died young.

Tamura Ryuichi

Ooka Makoto

The Sunken Cathedral

humans throughout the world seek proof of death. not
one, however, has ever witnessed death. humans after all
may be mere illusions, and reality their highest common
factor. objects supplant humans and begin their own in-
quisition. about life, about their own existence. even if a
chair asks a question, I must be fearful. reality may be the
least common multiple of those objects. incidentally, if
one is unable to feel anguish about the fate of man, how
can one risk one's own life in this world of upheaval? at
times geniuses have appeared, but all they achieved was to
refine nihilism further. obvious truth has merely intensi-
fied the gyration of white daylight.

he may have been trying to tell me something. but I shall
record only facts. as if first breaking at his knees he knelt
on the ground and fell. among the people who rushed to
him was a young man, just about my age, who mumbled

in spite of himself: "what a beautiful face, to make matters worse he trusts the world like a flower!"

—Tamura Ryuichi

With razor-sharp sensitivity Tamura Ryuichi mirrored in his work the nihilistic and desperate vein of the genre of modern Japanese poetry prevalent in our post-WWII society. His work crystallizes, with incomparable clarity of vision, an acute convergence of the spirit of the times and his poetic inspiration. He contributed to the establishment of the mores of our post-WWII poetry at its earliest stage in a most inimitable manner.

He was part of the Arechi [Wasteland] group, whose members included Miyoshi Toyoichiro, Ayukawa Nobuo, Kitamura Taro as well as Nakagiri Masao, Kurada Saburo, Kihara Koichi, and Yoshimoto Takaaki. The Arechi Group published the first group of anthologies, *Arechi Poems*, in August of 1951, which established an epoch-making milestone in our postwar poetry. Prior to this publication, the group had published a coterie magazine of the same title, *Arechi*, whose first issue appeared in September, 1947. But this was in turn a revival of the magazine, *Arechi*, which had been published during WWII.

How young poets (and wannabe's) fared during the war is difficult to trace at this point in time. They all faced the Pacific War as they became eligible for the draft, and with very few exceptions they were drafted and sent to the battleground. Some were killed in the war. Their war-time experiences from their teen years to their early twenties were absorbed into their post-WWII existence, and both shaped their concept of reality.

In this sense, their output was not simply derived from post-WWII elements. In fact, the core members of Arechi had already formed the group around 1940. Many Arechi members were generally under the influence of the pretensions of so-called modernism, even though they were the first wave of writers who insightfully captured the nihilistic frame of mind after WWII. Tamura wrote about their early activities in vivid detail in seven monthly installments in the poetry magazine *Eureka* from August 1960 through February 1961, which he titled "Young Arechi."

Of the group, Tamura was one of the most gravely afflicted by "pretentious" modernism. In the 7th installment of "Young Arechi," he described his work as "poems (?) reminiscent of the world of a retarded child," as evidenced by "The Legend of a Ghost," which he wrote when he was 17, as well as a few poems he published in the magazine *New Country*, the stronghold of modernism in Japan back then. It should be noted that Tamura was five years younger than Kuroda Saburo, four years younger than Nakagiri Masao, three years younger than Miyoshi Toyoichiro and Ayukawa Nobuo. Three or four years' difference was then a much more significant discrepancy in age than we can now imagine.

While Tamura was still writing poems which Miyoshi Toyoichiro put down as "tenderfoot modernism," Ayukawa Nobuo, for example, had begun to write poetry of despair and dark premonition, a type of pain-filled lament, clearly and definitively breaking away from then-prevalent "modernistic style." Therefore, it is not fair to say that the writings of "Young Arechi" members as a group were uniformly poisoned by a peculiarly jovial and flippant imitation of [European] modernism. However, before they could construct a truly new stage in the history of Japanese poetry, they had to experience a series of extremely rapid changes taking place over a short span of time. These included the deteriorating war situation, separations and isolation, bombing and destruction, the nation's defeat, the resulting destitution, and a totally overturned value system.

In regard to where the Arechi group stands, their inevitable emergence, and its significance, Yoshimoto Takaaki writes as follows:

In order for a poet to qualify to be called a post-war poet he would have had to internally pursue the meaning of having been forced to live through war-torn destruction, to endure the urgent sense of being stripped of his life, and then to experience the realities of devastation after the defeat . . . The poets of this generation directly experienced and survived extreme conditions before and during the war with an intense awareness of the individual self. But their expectations of being mentally liberated at the time of the defeat in the war were painfully shattered as mere illusions. The imperial system was preserved, the ruling class continued to rule, forgeries prevailed, and dejected veterans, hiding their injuries, emerged as liberators. Not a single fraction of hope was left, and no light of dawn emerged from anywhere across the social horizon of utter destruction and impoverishment.

In view of the realities of the time and its conditions it was inevitable that the Arechi group came to take up the central burden of post-war Japanese poetry, as they were exceptionally introspective in their poetic stance, principled in terms of their views of reality, and classic in their techniques. ("The Post-WWII Poets")

While Yoshimoto thus gave credit to the Arechi group, he fiercely criticized "the democratic literature movement where its participants simply viewed post-WWII Japanese society as liberation from the Imperialistic war, and attempted to start up by psychologically breaking away from their experiences before and during the war." In his critical views Yoshimoto stood on the same ground as Ayukawa Nobuo, who was the central theorist of the Arechi group. Consistent throughout the essays Ayukawa wrote around 1950 are his bitter denunciations of the desperate state of reality and his ironical paeans to the disillusionment felt by a generation who came to realize that the defeat was not liberation at all.

Such psychological phases of the Arechi group are most distinctly crystallized in Tamura's poetry during this period. Only a few years after he was derided for writing "tenderfoot modernism," Tamura showed himself as a strikingly different poet, transformed to the extent that one wonders how on earth he was able to achieve such a drastic metamorphosis. In his essay, "The Mapless Journey," he wrote,

I believe what is most important for a poet is the point in time and place at which he discovers his own archetypal poem. That is because this archetype represents the entirety of the "mapless journey" he is destined to take, and contains therein all concepts of time, death, and love as a single entity. It seems to me that a poet perilously travels through the discovery and re-discoveries of the archetype, and his journey takes the form of battles against his own archetype.

If I follow his manner of speaking, he discovered the poem that was to become his archetype in the devastation of Tokyo within two or three years after the defeat in the war. (As to the thought "what is most important for a poet is the point in time and place at which he discovers his own archetypal poem," it offers room for further examination and discussion. It may be stating his tendency toward classicism, or expressing a static view of poetry. This, in view of the waves of movements as a whole in post-WWII poetry over a dozen years, with the Arechi group as the first wave, would point to various interesting issues in our post-WWII poetry. But this is not a place for that discussion.)

"The Sunken Cathedral" was written around 1947. Just by reading this poem, one cannot determine why Tamura gave this poem a title similar to Debussy's, but there is certainly a contrapuntal equilibrium between the title and the poem.

This poem is difficult to explicate. It plays out collisions between logic and anti-logic, or reason and anti-reason, and in some sense poetry is inside those collisions themselves. The first part and the second part are not side by side on the same dimension. The poem, severed in two by a single blank line, is like two flat planes vertically interplaying with each other. And what the poet attempts to communicate to the reader is a certain psychological space, or an invisible space formed by the interplay between these two planes. The cool and strained logical statement of the first part and dramatic movements of the actors in the second part are brilliantly connected and contrasted by a technique similar to a cinematic flashback.

This poem, of course, is not attempting to express a defined idea, nor is it trying to communicate a certain emotion. What Tamura is trying to create is a shock, in a manner of speaking, nothing more and nothing less. In other words, it is not something that permeates and dissolves into the inner world of the reader, but rather it gives a physical shock to the reader's psyche like an external injury, so to speak, and as it sustains its force of impact the wound keeps throbbing without diminution or dissolution. The fundamental poetic substance this poem is intended to communicate is a voiceless scream. While the logical statement of the first part and dramatic action of the second part each maintains and presents its own inherent meaning, in the end, in order to give birth to this ultimate shock, both are mobilized to execute their roles through interplay with each other.

That is why this poem is structured in two layers—or rather three layers. Where the first part and the second part collide with each other generates an invisible crash, creating the most important third element, that is, the eternal state of shock. This state of shock may be described in various ways, such as disillusionment with post-WWII reality, total sense of loss, or hopelessness. But what Tamura has created here is the shock only these words could produce, not a reproduction of a certain specific condition. In other words, it is the shock of a different dimension created only with words: a new reality produced by pure imagination. The construction of an imaginative reality has become a property of Japanese post-WWII poetry as a whole, and it is now so prevalent as to need no mention. But we must acknowledge the fact that the poets of the Arechi group, most notably Tamura, played a crucial part in establishing this trend.

Tamura, having created his explosive style as a superb reflection of the post-WWII situation, achieved similar types of expression in a number of poems during this period of time, and became the most discerning forger of the post-war sense of despair and the void. They include several published in *Arechi Poems 1951*: "Poetry and Poetics about a Slope," "Witness," "Etching," "Autumn," "Voice," "Golden Fantasy," "Winter Music," "Emperor," "Reunion," "Room," "1940s/Summer," "Images," and "Noon." Some of these may not yet have crystallized his own unique poetic expression, but as a whole they had a deep, striking, and remarkable impact. Surely Tamura was about to discover "a poem that can be his own archetype."

NOON

what exists outside the window
fire, rock, bones,
our "time" carved into teeth, nails, and hair,
amid a shower of rain, premonitions and intimations,
    dangling from a bed
is her arm

what exists outside the window,
it does not die,
it is not part of history,
a single scream—directed at whom?
a single scar—what destructive meaning does it have?
who will injure her arm
what exists outside the window!

she is ill. does that mean
she loves me?
her call to me, a single call, just once,
creates shade in a vast desert, and now
the world enters noon

What is "Noon"? It makes me think of a mindscape, a curiously bright emptiness, where time is arrested, every relationship severed, leaving every "thing" simply there, isolated. And what Tamura is trying to capture is precisely a time and space of that kind.

When he talks about what exists outside the window, perhaps the window is also his own eye. In other words, what exists outside the window is what exists outside of his mind. It is nothing but the world that spurns the autonomous participation of the poet's psyche, the world of things that exist without him. In this world only fire, rock, bones, teeth, and hair exist as remnants of human existence. In this world "time," having been deprived of the motion that is its essence, carved into its fragments and parts, simply remains in stasis, rather than ticking on inside us as it should. In this listless noon "amid a shower of rain, premonitions, and intimations," only a woman's arm dangling from a bed is alive. She is lying in bed because she is ill. Then who is this woman? In view of Tamura's other work, this woman represents modern European civilization on the verge of its collapse, the totality of various things Tamura has treasured and loved, and she might even be a real woman. No matter. The woman is certainly the only presence soft to the touch in this barren noon, the world of endlessly bright vacuity. That she is soft to the touch means she is alive. Unlike fire, rock, or bones, she is living and she is ill. Being ill is the wretched proof of being alive. In this paradoxical perception of life lies a characteristic of Tamura's poetry as well as that of a number of post-WWII poets.

Following this, the poet expresses his perverse desire to trigger resurrection by definitively killing off both various attributes of humans already turned into mere "things" and a certain precious truth lying in sick bed. "[What] exists outside the window" is a mere meaningless "thing" that cannot even die, and therefore it is not "part of history." As such we cannot damage it, and it is totally indifferent to us. So might she be. But only she shows proof of being alive by virtue of being ill. The two lines "she is ill. does that mean / she loves me?" are on one level totally conceptual, but given what we discussed above, we realize that they represent a desperate yearning for life. This is somewhat quixotic and self-delusional, but the poet is deeply hurt by what one might call the impenetrability of a world in which he cannot participate on his own terms. The world is in front of him, indifferent, spurning him. Needless to say, in such a relationship between the world and an individual, whether one wishes to maintain or break the relationship, one is forced to execute extremely abstract maneuvers.

In great measure the ferocious force of impact in Tamura's poetry during this period originates from such abstract postures. Consider the core of the shock in "The Sunken Cathedral," and the fierce thirst for life in "Noon." They are both rooted in the same psyche. After he shaped an era with a series of such pieces, Tamura wrote longer poems, such as "Standing Coffin." These are considered his representative poems, and successfully give an even more enduring voice to his unique psyche, which had already been presented in his own inimitable style in his earlier work. However, as he achieved stylistic brilliance in his expression, ironically, his achievement turned out to portend a dry spell. Poetic aesthetics is not sufficient to accommodate vacuity after all.

For some time since, Tamura has not published notable poems, but recently he is again immersing himself in poetry. I find "World Without Words" very exciting as it shows Tamura in a new stance in which he delves into the world without words, that is, paradoxically the essence of poetry itself, having come through a universe of words generated from the images of post-WWII.

(1963, *Japanese Literature: Analysis and Criticism*)

[poems and essay trans. Takako Lento]

Renowned Japanologist Donald Keene called OOKA MAKOTO (b. 1931) "perhaps the finest [critic of poetry] in Japan today." As a notable poet in his own right, Ooka combines in his criticism a deep understanding of poetic impulses with literary and historical perspectives. Among his many literary awards and medals of honor in Japan and abroad is *L'ordre national de la legion d'honneur* from France.

In the Beginning Was the Fear

Miho Nonaka

I first read "Four Thousand Days and Nights" by Tamura Ryuichi in a pocketsize anthology of modern Japanese poetry. Compiled by the Japan P.E.N. Club, *Kotobayo hanasake* (*Let Words Bloom*) was one of the hundred recommended books for young and aspiring minds in the early 1990's. I had just transferred from a Japanese high school to an American school in Tokyo. I carried the anthology with me as an anchor to the outside world when, each morning, I had to enter this Japanese "Little America," where two languages clashed daily and no one spoke pure English nor Japanese (if language is capable of being pure, that is).

Ooka Makoto, the editor of this anthology, calls "Four Thousand Days and Nights" a "shock," and that's what it was to my ear. The poem stood relentlessly against what I had understood to be the basic traits of Japanese poetry: the pathos of life, intetextuality, the modulation of odd-numbered syllables, etc. From the beginning, it was like listening to some apocalyptic news report translated from another language:

In order for a poem to be born
we must kill
we must kill many
we shoot down, assassinate, poison many we love

Even though such insistent commands to destroy for the sake of creating a single poem struck me as absurd, at that particular time I could intuit a feeling of crisis behind the poem's dry, uninflected tone. Lack of emotion could result from too much of it, in cases of intense grief or fear. Crisis speaks to crisis. And perhaps, the voice of a poet whose imagination focuses on a single, extreme crisis carries far. Like Paul Celan's "Death Fugue," where milk turns black and night is day, Tamura's haunting incantation conjures up a negative space, a total inversion of light and dark, life and death.

*

Even before "Four Thousand Days and Nights," Tamura had discovered his style through writing a prose poem titled "Etching." His essay, "Nikutai ha kanashii" ("The Flesh Is Sad"), tells us that it was the first work born of what he calls his "fierce intent to *compose* 'poetry,'" as opposed to a mere experiment. To Tamura, the fact that "Etching" took the form of a prose poem points to a kind of "despair" he had previously felt towards "poetry," or the ingrained idea of his native poetic tradition. "You could also call it my *shyness* with 'poetry'," he adds (indeed, he feels so shy that he has to put quotation marks around the word "poetry" each time he uses it in this essay).

Although his equation of "despair" with "shyness" is puzzling at first, I recognize a similarly mixed feeling of both pessimism and embarrassment in the works of Japanese modernists before World War II, when they felt compelled to start writing deliberately against the personal lyricism of their predecessors. One of the most influential poets to young Tamura was Nishiwaki Junzaburo (1894-1982), known as the godfather of Japanese surrealism, and Nishiwaki wrote his first poems in English, French and Latin, because of his uneasiness with, and particular distaste for, the traditional Japanese lyric mode.

Tamura didn't start writing in a foreign tongue, but it is worth noting that the very first poem he would call his own was given a title in the language of translation. How he first encountered the foreign word "etching" is unclear, even to himself. "Was it when I was drinking the low-grade moonshine in Shinbashi's black market after I returned from the war?" Tamura asks in his essay. He can only speculate that "It must have been some time during those seven years of MacArthur's Japanese Occupation."

The Japanese word for "etching" consists of three kanji characters. It is a modern invention, an avant-garde effort to naturalize a European phrase by combining Chinese pictograms. By choosing these picturesque characters instead of phonetic kana script, Tamura clearly intends the title of his poem to be a visual experience. The first is 腐, meaning to rot or decay, followed by 刻, to cut or chisel, and ending with 画 for painting. Tamura recounts how he was "moved to *pain*" on his first encounter with 腐刻画. The character 腐 contains the radical for flesh 肉 in it, and it evokes the surface made of flesh instead of metal, being cut into by means of corrosive memory and spreading a leafy pattern of tremulous rust. Tamura writes: "The moment I came upon the word '腐刻画,' the still undifferentiated vortex inside me began developing a dark green image with both cadence and colors so that it inevitably took this 'poetic' shape."

Moreover, the original poem appears in all vertical lines, following traditional Japanese writing conventions. One of Tamura's English translators, Christopher Drake, compares the poet's lines to the "girders unsettling in high wind," and in the case of "Etching," they are arranged in two uneven, perpendicular stanzas.

A slim space between the two is where "my 'poem' happens," explains Tamura, "I could even say that the true aim of this piece was to *introduce* a severance and a blank." In his published interview titled "Kyofu, fuan, yumoa" ("Fear, Anxiety, Humor"), Tamura also acknowledges that what interests the poet the most is a gap: "I want to write a poem where the blank between lines becomes a deep valley." Readers must leap from one line to another at the risk of "falling in the middle with eyes closed," which might require an extra measure of "crawling up from the bottom" before moving on to the next line. Tamura timidly adds that this is nothing but a poetic ideal, his New Year's "dream" as opposed to resolution.

"Etching" is Tamura's cornerstone poem in that this is where Tamura *willed* his voice to begin its precarious action forward by leaping between vertical lines, stanzas, and shifting landscapes (from "an ancient city" to "a modern precipice," from "night" to "daybreak"). For Tamura, the fact that he was born a year after the publication of T. S. Eliot's *The Waste Land* holds special significance, because it speaks for his sense of belatedness as a poet; "the world was already *wasteland*" before he had ever taken any part in it. Tamura is a post-Eliotic, post-WWII Arechi (Wasteland) poet born in "the eastern capital of Japan," and as such, he was doomed to start writing poetry as a combination of foreign prose and an acrobatic performance between the vertical acts of creation and destruction, propelled by his oft-mentioned theme of "fear."

In the same interview, Tamura insists on the difference between fear and anxiety. After admitting that "fear" has been the consistent motivation for his composition, the poet observes the current poetic trend in comparison: "The main motif of works by the so-called 'contemporary poets' is *anxiety*." He goes on to argue that the driving force of anxiety is "desire," because, simply put, without desire and want, there would be neither anxiety nor discontent. In comparison, Tamura senses that what constitutes the foundation of his fear is not desire. While conceding that many great contemporary works are based on anxiety, he also suggests: "There needs to be more poems written based on the very fear of human existence itself." And yet, to be completely rid of desire goes counter to the human instinct for self-preservation. To claim such an absolute notion of fear is to acknowledge a tunnel or vacuum inside us, where we become alienated not only from the rest of the humanity, but also from ourselves, our very existence.

Perhaps, it is this fear that caused a split between "he" and "I" at the beginning of Tamura's poetic production. In "Etching," what comes after the stanza break—a narrow valley where the life of the poem has already transpired—is dire news brought by the first person "I": "He, namely the man I have begun to tell you about, killed his father when he was young. That autumn his mother went beautifully mad." The sudden introduction of "I" reporting the action of "He" is unquestionably jarring. Why does the poet choose to call attention to the staged gap between the main agent in the poem and its omniscient narrator?

In his autobiographical notes, "10 Kara kazoete" ("Counting from 10"), Tamura brings up this question, "Why did the 3rd-person 'he' appear?" He follows it by suggesting, "I probably needed a pair of eyes other than my own." If the original source of his writing were "the very fear of human existence itself," it would be impossible to confront such a level of fear for long without distancing oneself from it, objectifying it or turning to irony as a recourse. Even if a poet could, his writing career would be a brief one. In "Fear, Anxiety, Humor," Tamura admits that he must secure some outside, realistic point of reference at all costs, because "I would be a dead man if I kept on composing with the same method I had used in 'Four Thousand Days and Nights,'" the poem I had once depended on as a teenager for the very reason that it fiercely and methodically rejects all familiar and everyday things in order to turn one's mind into "a state of vacuum."

In his notes, Tamura offers a revealing statement: "My subsequent books of poetry would tell you how the 'he' who appears in this poem and 'I' would fare." Another prose poem "Sunken Temple" has a similar structure to "Etching" in that it consists of two stanzas and it is only in the second stanza that we discover the dual existence of the first-person "I" and the third-person "he." How do they "fare" in this poem? I will quote the poem's entire second stanza below:

he may have tried to tell me something. but I shall record only facts. as if breaking at his knees first he kneeled on the ground and fell. among the people who rushed to him was a young man, just about my age, who mumbled in spite

of himself: "what a beautiful face, to make matters worse
he trusts the world like a flower!"

Here, the characters are not only "he" and "I," since Tamura
introduces yet another persona, "a young man, just about my age,"
who allows the poet to draw even more distance from the immedi-
ate impression of the first-person "I." The relationship between
"he" and "I" becomes triangulated, and the final exclamatory re-
mark, "what a beautiful face, to make matters worse he trusts the
world like a flower!" belongs to this twice-removed persona.

The expression "like a flower" is a cliché. A beautiful woman
would have a "flowerlike" face, or in a romantic tale, such a woman
would laugh "like a flower." 花 (flower) is a traditional image in clas-
sical Japanese poetry, where the word almost exclusively refers to
cherry blossoms. Their fleeting beauty has long been an established
metaphor for the brevity of human life, and the image of the scat-
tering petals often symbolizes honorable, sacrificial death of the
samurai or the souls of the war dead.

In "Sunken Temple," Tamura uses this conventional phrase to
present the flowerlike innocence and belief of the character "he,"
forming a sharp contrast to the darkly pessimistic first stanza ("ge-
niuses did sometimes appear, but all they did was to further refine
nihilism"). Furthermore, against his postmodernist grain, Tamura
includes a generic (and often subjective) adjective "beautiful" to
qualify the face of the poet's alter ego. The idea is carried over from
the earlier poem "Etching," where "his mother went *beautifully*
mad." Of course, the coupling of beauty with insanity or the image
of blind acceptance of the world as pretty flora is meant to be
ironic.

If "Etching" and "Sunken Temple" are both derived from "the
very fear of human existence itself" in Tamura's words, would the
poet be able to distance himself from its ruthless gravity by speak-
ing through the masks of personae or protect himself by being
lightly armed with irony? Part of me resists the idea that Tamura's
taste for irony and absurdity is all there is in these instances. If the
poems have more to do with the absolute nature of fear than the

relative quality of desire-driven anxiety, the original meaning of the word 美 (beauty) must retain some of its force in these poems like a handsomely etched scar, and we are to take its image, at least partially, at its face value.

In the notes provided by Christopher Drake who translated the poem's title as "Sunken Cathedral" instead of "Sunken Temple," we find the original title "沈める寺" is a Japanese translation of Debussy's *La cathédrale engloutie*, a prelude for solo piano. Like "Etching," the poem gets its title from an impression of a foreign phrase translated into the poet's native tongue. Drake adds a telling comment in his notes: "[Tamura], and many of his generation, once believed that beauty was stronger than death—World War II changed that."

I doubt that the poem has much to do with the musical composition itself. Rather, Tamura must have been drawn to the image its title suggests. The dreamlike combination of the words "cathedral" and "engulfed" evokes such tragic grandeur of a sinking city (Drake also notes that for Tamura, the archetypal European city was Venice) that it becomes an appropriate entrance into the poem built on fear, void and marred beauty. Moreover, in my view, the original title "沈める寺" has a visual significance similar to the case of "腐刻画" ("Etching"). It seems more than just a coincidence that the pictograph for poetry is 詩, made of two radicals for 言 (speech) and 寺 (temple). What becomes drowned in Tamura's poem "沈める寺" ("Sunken Temple") is not only the architectural beauty of the European ideal and metaphysics, but also the symbolic status of his native poetic tradition. Words are no longer capable of building a house of worship where the sacred—be it truth or beauty—dwells.

As for the question of housing his own Muse, Tamura starts "Gods of Poetry" by locating the gods of Saito Mokichi (1882-1953), the renowned tanka poet of the Araragi school:

Mokichi's gods of poetry
  were the Asakusa Kannon and broiled eels

Because he walled his poems with solid form
he only had to go to the temple's Thunder Gate

The "solid form" refers to traditional tanka prosody of thirty-one syllables in five lines. While Saito Mokichi was able to find his gods of poetic inspiration in the classical structure preceding haiku, Tamura's "nervous gods of poetry" keep "pacing, pacing" without "fire insurance." Whatever the force that drives Tamura's poetic production is, it's clearly restless, fearful and unpredictable; his spooked muse of free verse must break away from the age-old pattern of alternating between five and seven syllables. This simply means that the poet is guaranteed no "insurance" throughout his writing career, no tradition to fall back on in case of a burning disaster.

In contrast with the prescribed temple of tanka and the energy-giving eels (a delicacy often associated with building stamina for the summer), Tamura's gods are given no established residence for public ceremonies, and the poet is more likely to turn to whisky than to nutritious fish for poetic inspiration (during the University of Iowa's International Writing Program in 1967-68, Tamura infamously sold their gift of library books in order to buy himself a bottle). The concluding couplet of "Gods of Poetry" leaves Tamura's brand of poetic deities with: "Small houses / large silences."

In the interview "Fear, Anxiety, Humor," Tamura illustrates the reality of a poem by using the image of a house. The only thing that secures the poem's life is the structured space of the work itself. He speaks for the Japanese poets of his generation: "Because we don't work with the traditional form, after making one house, we must tear it down and start building yet another house." It is a risky business, similar to the idea of trapezing between the vertical lines and deep valleys of a poem. "In that sense," admits Tamura, "I envy those who write using traditional prosody . . . in haiku or tanka, once you are satisfied with the finished house, you can keep building according to the same room arrangement and floor plan."

For Japanese poets, free verse meant breaking away not from meter or rhyme, but from the cadence established by the familiar chain of five and seven syllables. As T. S. Eliot wrote, "No verse is free for the man who wants to do a good job," and Tamura insists that however small or spontaneous the style of your house may be, it must work as a house, where you can eat and sleep under a roof, protected from the outside world against the "large silences" that surround or pervade the humble houses of poetry. "Gotta try and try, you know?" he advises. Free verse "can have only one room or it can be radically simplified and rational in its design like Bauhaus," Tamura asserts, offering the one caveat that "you cannot call it 'a new house,' however; if you have only built a wall, it has no functions of a house."

In Tamura's later verse, we find its relentless, vertical mode of building and demolishing shifting to the seemingly lighter and flatter tone of a "retired" master poet; its sensibility is reminiscent of the Rakugo comedy tradition and humorous literature from the Edo period (1603-1868). Tamura's grandfather, a true-born Edokko (named after Edo, premodern Tokyo), is said to have educated his grandson's ear to the speech rhythms, sensual humor and pathos of Japan's pre-Westernized age where people referred to the city's frequent fires and street fights as "the flowers of Edo."

Nevertheless, Tamura's very first notion of his own poetry came from a place foreign and removed enough to protect him from his deep-seated embarrassment at overt lyricism and old sentimentality. His project of continually moving forward by leveling the finished house and starting anew began with "腐刻画," an etched innerscape and a rusting, greenish scar. The title stands as a memento to an anonymous effort to translate and internalize the foreign art form and its injurious beauty.

Japanese critics repeatedly point out that the foundational principle of the Arechi (Wasteland) group had already been postwar even before the actual war literally turned their native land into a waste. And yet, truly original Arechi poems (and not half-baked imitations of European modernism) weren't born until after the Second World War. Like "the fears of one stray dog" in "Four Thousand Days and Nights," who "sees what our eyes do not see" and "hears what our ears do not hear," Tamura's fears were awakened as he roamed through a wasteland of what once had been his hometown. He had to turn to poetry to "*introduce* a severance and a blank" on the page, to build his lines around deep valleys and fashion his poems into sunken temples. Like the high-spirited townsmen of Edo, who lived without much furniture under the constant threat of devastating fires, Tamura never saw a permanent home in poetic structures; rather, he chose a state of being balanced between destruction and creation, doing and undoing, as he survived Japan's postwar era where the distinction between being alive and being spiritually dead became increasingly obscure.

(2010)

MIHO NONAKA is a bilingual writer born and raised in Tokyo. Her first book of Japanese poems, *Garasu no tsuki*, was a finalist for Japan's national poetry prize. Her poetry and nonfiction in English have appeared widely in publications including *Ploughshares*, *Quarterly West*, *Iowa Review*, *Cimarron Review*, and *Tin House*. She is Assistant Professor of English and Creative Writing at Wheaton College.

A Journey to Fear

Ayukawa Nobuo

I believe what is most important for a poet is the point in time and place at which he discovers his own archetypal poem. That is because this archetype represents the entirety of the "mapless journey" he is destined to take, and contains therein all concepts of time, death and love as a single entity. It seems to me that a poet perilously travels through the discovery and re-discoveries of the archetype, and his journey takes the form of battles against his own archetype.[1]

To a poet, imagination is the energy that ceaselessly stimulates and re-creates his passion. Unless this energy is persistently maintained, the pathway of a poet's inner passion will not evolve. As C. Day Lewis also advises, "To fortify imagination, write poetry." In order to discipline their imagination, painters paint pictures, and composers write music. The disciplined imagination will further cultivate the inner

---

[1] From "Mapless Journey."

pathway for a poet, a painter and a musician, and push forth a new life. Here lies a furious interaction between the energy and his technique.[2]

These two short quotes are excerpts from Tamura's recent essays. Both of these, I believe, give us important clues to his poetry and poetics.

In the first quote, he likens a poet's work to a "mapless journey," but not all poets set out on their journeys without a map. Rather, we might say that no other time in history has seen so much trust in cheap, color-coded, unreliable maps as ours.

Generally most people do not feel the world where we live and die to be "perilous and unknown," and seem to trust their guides and maps.

However, if one perceives this world as something like the "Dark Continent," dangerous and uncharted, where one is forced to tread further into the deep of the Continent under relentless caution and tension, it is quite doubtful that commercially available maps would help.

For a traveler through the Dark Continent, maps are misleading. It often happens, in fact, that he loses his way in the jungle, even though he has found his pathway on a map.

But a poet is not like a blundering traveler, because he does not do a thing like looking at reality after consulting a map. Under all circumstances he tries to find his way only in reality.

In this context it probably won't be difficult to understand the progress of Tamura's work through this metaphor of a "mapless journey."

Actually Tamura originally used this metaphor quite artfully, borrowing the idea from a book by Graham Greene, to explain my attitude toward poetry. So I am returning the favor by applying it to his poetry. But before I proceed, I would like to explain why we need to go on a "mapless journey."

In the essay from which the passage above is quoted, Tamura writes: "What did our civilization destroy most on this earth, having

---

[2] From "A Roadside Pigeon."

had to go through two world wars over half a century? We can name many things such as uncountable people's lives, huge masses of materials, many cities, temples or churches, and others. However, if you are a poet, you'd name words and imagination."

It is significant that he brings up two world wars and suggests that they destroyed our words and imagination. At a cursory glance this statement may sound quite ordinary, but he is pointing to something very important which we must not miss.

That is to say, since our civilization first saw world-scale war, we have gone through two such conflicts. As a result our "words and imagination" can no longer easily reach the world of understanding and love. In other words, "the world" that was originally perceived as being for the light of love and understanding has been completely inverted to "total darkness" by the wars. This misfortune rendered modern man's inner life into disastrous ruins, worse even than the physical devastation brought about by destructive wars. As we try to understand our poetic mindscape and linguistic structure, we must not forget that we first came to know the sense of "the world" through the World War, and that it came accompanied with innumerable images of misery.

If "words and imagination" are what the wars destroyed most completely, isn't that destruction still going on? Common sense about poetry has it that if even a single word is marred in a poem, the orderliness of all the words is disturbed. In our world, aren't an infinite number of words already marred?

Given the condition of the world we are in, it is not strange that a poet's views of things, his sensitivities, and his imagination have changed to be totally different from those of the past. To start with, the criteria for evaluating poetry have changed, and so have our views on the forms of poetry. And a poet in the new era tries to find a new form for words appropriate to the modes of his own creative sensitivities.

Thus, a poet has no choice but to embark on a "mapless journey." Of course nothing assures the security of his endeavor. However, for a poet who has intuitively recognized the world to be "perilous and unknown," no amount of "assurance of security" will be enough to rest his soul. He will spur himself to take off on his mapless journey.

Tamura's prose poetry, starting with *Poetry and Poetics Relating to Slope* after the end of WWII, presents a style most acutely responsive to these circumstances. For example, "Etching," the earliest of the poems in this book, consists of two stanzas:

He sees, in front of him, a landscape like one he saw in a German etching. It seems like a bird's-eye view of an ancient city, which is about to shift from evening into night, or like a realistic picture representing a modern precipice that is changing from deep night into daybreak.

He, namely the man I have begun to tell you about, killed his father when he was young. That autumn his mother went beautifully mad.

Just think that for this type of poetry to appear, we had to experience two world wars. If we agree that this work was not conceivable at least prior to 1945, we will find it much easier to go deeper into this poem.

On the surface this poem says nothing about wars. Some may wonder how this is impacted by WWII.

But try to compare this poem with any written prior to 1945, and you'll find that the fundamental differences in the formative conditions of those poems have to be traced back to the two world wars. Of course, "Etching" is a poem no one but Tamura could write in any time or place, but this poem owes its indelible shape to the horrific vision that is only conceivable at "this time and place" after WWII.

After WWI, we encoountered dada, surrealism, imagism and such. We also saw new movements such as futurism and expressionism. And as we all know, various types of new poetry were written, breaking away from the literary conventions of the times. However, the literary environment that supported these spectacular new movements did not offer conditions mature enough to produce Tamura's "Etching" and the series of prose poems that followed. That is to say, Tamura's prose poems would not have been possible without the experiences of WWII.

To understand this better, compare pre-WWII poets' work,

such as the poetry and prose of Takahashi Shinkichi and the prose poems of Kitagawa Fuyuhiko or Hishiyama, Shuzo with those of Tamura's. The difference will be instantly clear.

The definitive difference between Tamura and the poets of the preceding generation forcefully manifests itself in his creative sensitivity. In terms of his sense of "time," and his sense of equilibrium between images, he is more scrutinizing and focused than any of the poets of the preceding generation. He also has a unique ability (also his natural disposition) in his mind's capacity to take what he perceives and senses from the outside world (→ single words) and rearrange and re-construct them in the world of his imagination. He deals with multi-dimensional space according to his own laws of perspective, which suggests an unusually penetrating intellect. But the most riveting aspect of his poetry lies in his vision of blood-freezing fear accentuated with strong emotions. And the lines of his poetry, generated from the equilibrium of intellect and sensibility, are so magnificent as to be incomparable.

These characteristics of Tamura's poetry reach a certain pinnacle in a series called "A Visionary." Here he shows us, through highly developed poetic techniques, how he feels about this world we live in, and what kind of vision he has of it. We should note in particular how meticulous—how precise the application of linguistic rules—his poetic technique is in presenting his own vision.

In my view, his extraordinarily far-reaching perspective, his destructive vision, his concept of death and so forth in "A Visionary" are the product of a sharply honed creative sensitivity specially accorded to a man who is on a "mapless journey" through a pitch-black world. Accordingly, his nervous system and emotional make-up are somewhat different from those of poets who are following proven courses that rely on maps, and when we read his individual poems, some give us problems in understanding his intent or purposes.

However, I believe when we stand at a vantage point where we can survey the entirety of his poetry, we will clearly carve onto our minds the significance of each of his poems, which are the pillars supporting his totality. As Oliver Wendell Holmes said, ". . . as I review each decade, I find some new pieces falling into their appropriate places . . ."

The title poem, "Four Thousand Days and Nights," was written when the author happened to be at that particular vantage point. This poem captures, in a flash of intellectual-emotional white heat, the decade-long torment experienced by the poet's soul as it was reborn from the ashes after WWII, and shows the transference of its idiosyncratic empirical significance from negative energy to positive.

However, when we read the first and the fifth stanza, which provide the underlying meaning of the poem,

> In order for a poem to be born
> we must kill
> we must kill many
> we shoot down, assassinate, poison many we love
> ....
> In order to give birth to a poem
> we must kill those we love
> that is the only way to resurrect the dead
> it is the path we must take

Ultimately the difference between these two stanzas comes down to the contrast between "for a poem to be born," and "to give birth to a poem." Even assuming we understand this transference of meaning, still some of us might feel the word "to kill" sounds too drastic. In fact, "to kill" is more specifically expressed as "shoot down," "assassinate," and "poison" in the larger structure. While the first and the fifth stanzas form the poem's wings, the second, third and fourth stanzas provide patterns of images, and the poem's overall resonance feels sadistic and sensational.

Having said that, a similar resonance consistently echoes through the rhythms of most of his poetry. We might say it happens to be concentrated in the powerful word "kill" in this case. And I must pay special attention to the significance of the word "kill" in this particular poem.

The meaning of this word is extremely difficult to fathom, and what I am going to say includes my own dogmatic speculation, so I am not sure if I am correct. But, I dare say, it means that only through the most destructive and negative actions can an individual save those dear to his heart. At the bottom of this poem lies the weight of the unreasonableness of this world, an utter distrust of human actions and the like, and that seems to form the basis of his idea of "resurrecting the dead."

In order to understand this more clearly, I would like to see what "death" means to Tamura by examining "Standing Coffin," his representative poem. Tamura offers his own explication of this poem:

"'Standing Coffin' signifies a certain world. In this poem consisting of three large stanzas I, II, and III, I tried to shed light on a certain world to show its significance from the viewpoint of the mind of the jobless, the exiled, and the sick. In a world where people cannot die, they cannot be alive either; in such a world an individual simply drifts among nameless multitudes, having been chased out from every room, every city, every land; in such a world 'you' and 'I' are merely variations of 'we.' This is my theme, as I was challenged by the term, 'Standing Coffin.'"

Reading the above, everyone will realize that "In a world where people cannot die, they cannot be alive either" is the fundamental thought that supports most of Tamura's poetic themes. Once we understand this, it is not difficult for us to see how the poet of "Four Thousand Days and Nights" confronts, with fierce anger, "the world where one cannot die"—a confrontation that is necessary to produce even a single poem. His vehement tone, urgent chasing rhythms, crisp and clear images, and a dynamic presentation of the ideas in his poetry, are due to his resolute posture in his fight against "the world where one cannot die," and not a product of mere rhetoric. From his early prose poems such as "Etching" and "The Sunken Cathedral" down to the relatively recent "Three Voices" and "The Thin Line," the poet has sustained his taut intensity, which proves to us that the poet possesses not only a sharp creative sensitivity, but also underlying unwavering convictions.

Why, then, does he feel this world to be "the world where one cannot die"? That is because, as symbolized in a most austere way in "Standing Coffin," we are intrinsically separated from our land, our home, and our work. These are represented respectively by the exiled, the sick, and the jobless.

In the world where we humans are born, raised and die, our land, our home and our work form what you might call the mother's womb for our emotions. But when we are cut off from it, our humanity necessarily becomes unstable. Those who lost their land, those who lost their home, and those who lost their work will end up being ghosts in the "drifting world" whether they like it or not.

And this "drifting world" is the origin of uneasiness, fear, and disease which threaten modern civilization from its foundation. "Standing Coffin" is a powerful poem in which Tamura squarely confronts and gouges out the gigantic evil of modern civilization and the modern world. It is a monumental work as post-WWII philosophical poetry.

> We have no venom
> We have no venom to heal us

Here again he is dreaming a fearful dream. His mind seems to be in a realm of mental science unimaginable to us, dreaming that we have "no venom" to heal "the incurably sick."

This poem, as a whole, is heavily pain-filled and cruel, and except for the two lines, "We have no love / All we have is the love of the sick" [only the love of the sick is in affirmative—note by this author], it offers no affirmative or comforting lines. No other poetry, it seems, ever so logically cornered the modern world and denied it so absolutely. This is a masterpiece, though I personally find it unpalatable, that I believe will be among the work that will surely survive generations from now.

The concept that not dying is not the same as "life" is not so new these days, given the influence of poetry by T. S. Eliot and others, but no other poet but Tamura, at least in Japan, has ever suggested so clearly and logically the world where one can die is equal to the place one can live, even though paradoxically.

Tamura's paradoxes are often grandiose yet unrecognizable, framed in a sort of strange world of logic, whose overall structure itself is the "inversion" of his logical structure. I clearly recall the time when I first read "Standing Coffin." It made me think of "demonology."

The framework for his vision is more or less the same in "Four Thousand Days and Nights" and "Standing Coffin." But in "Three Voices"[3] his vision breaks through the thick walls of logic.

> Upon hearing the voice
> I will finally give birth to Mother
> upon hearing the voice
> our corpses will assail vultures
>
> upon hearing the voice
> Mother will give birth to death

Here is a world no one can break. What we have here is neither logic nor anti-logic, neither vision nor reality, but something ultimately called poetry. Moreover, I believe these six lines present the point words and the creative imagination have reached in their progression as they rip through the ennui of this world and battle against its fear and terror. Of course such a world exists only as a metaphor.

To be honest, I am at a loss as to how to evaluate these lines. I surmise most everyone has the same view.

It will be best to leave it for history to judge. But I am also tempted to say that between these lines lurks the shadow of a critical finger pointing at our nuclear age, questioning how our history itself will be judged.

At any rate, Tamura Ryuichi is a poet's poet. It will be poets who ultimately know his worth and determine his reputation. From this perspective, it is not by chance that Tamura's theme in much of his poetry is poetry, such as "Poetry and Poetics Relating to Slope," "Four Thousand Days and Nights," "Three Voices," and "The Thin Line." "A Visionary" also suggests a poet, and one can safely say that the protagonists in his poetry are almost all poets.

No one has any doubt that the protagonist, the poet, is an excellent marksman with words, like the hunter in "The Thin Line."

> You pull the trigger
> I die in the middle of words

---

[3] Not included in this volume.

I believe anyone who has any interest in poetry in our modern time will be interested in this hunter's new game, and will pay a great deal of attention to how far he goes, and what he is after.

Fortunately, this hunter has not given up charging forward into the depths to hunt down big game. He has not abandoned his vision of achieving glory by way of fear. Given his constitution, he is showing astounding patience.

(1956, *Four Thousand Days and Nights*)

[trans. Takako Lento]

The poetry of AYUKAWA NOBUO (1920-86), the leader and chief theorist of the Arechi group, is heavily shadowed by the deaths of his friends in the war. It was his translation of T.S. Eliot's *The Waste Land* that so greatly influenced Tamura. Three years senior to Tamura, Ayukawa understood and appreciated Tamura's poetry probably better than any of their contemporaries. The Ayukawa Nobuo Award for poetry and criticism was established in 2010 to honor his achievements as a representative literary figure in post-WWII poetry.

Camel's Milk Cheese

Tanikawa Shuntaro

[Translator's note: In this essay the author poses as both interviewer and interviewee.]

—What do you think of Tamura?

What do I think of Tamura? That's a tough question. In a poem, Miyoshi Tatsuji[1] called [the poet] Sakutaro[2] a "personality I feel fond of," as you know. I have a similar feeling about Tamura. I feel a sort of fondness from a distance, like the feeling I get from looking at a camel in a zoo. You see, Tamura cuts an unarguably distinctive figure and we just let him be. Yet that figure does not fit in well in Japan now. It provokes a kind of humor, but at the same time generates some poignancy.

But while Sakutaro makes us believe that he wouldn't have fit

---

[1] Miyoshi Tatsuji (1900-1964), poet. Mr. Tanikawa is referring to Miyoshi's poem, "My Master, Hagiwara Sakutaro," an elegy upon Hagiwara's death, in which he wrote, "you were a poet, irreplaceable, supreme and unique."
[2] Hagiwara Sakutaro (1886-1942) was known for his masterful colloquial style in presenting emotional realities and extraordinary sensibilities.

in no matter what era he was born in, Tamura makes me feel that he might have lived happily, not as a poet, if he had been born in the late Tokugawa Era.[3] Of course, from his point of view, he may be enjoying himself pretty well even now. As you know Tamura is a drinker, and I am not. I cannot fully understand those who love to drink. But you see, he is a type who would inflict pain upon those who were close to him, because he seemed like he'd fade out of this world unless someone took care of him. Of course he might be just artful enough to make people feel that way.

When we toured the US together reading poetry, I'd be asked how I knew him. I'd respond, "His fourth wife was my first wife." People would look at me funny, but it was just the way it turned out to be, you see. Yet, when I'd see him later he'd earnestly say to me, "I am not a bad guy, you know," as if he had to make excuses, which amused me. Even in those instances, though, he was classy. I once read an occasional essay of his in which he likened his last wife and current wife to a fox and a badger. I was impressed then with how free from venom he is. In his day-to-day life, of course, he may be dealing with the ugliness of reality, but his writing has a distilled quality achieved through skill and effort.

—How do Tamura's real life and his work relate to each other?

I really don't know. I have a bad habit of getting interested in a writer's real life. To appreciate someone's work, reading it should be enough, but particularly with contemporary writers I tend to think of their work along with their real lives, or rather, how they live. It's not that how they live necessarily affects my appreciation of their work. It's just that I try to get closer to the work that way since I am always conscious of how my work relates to the way I live.

---

[3] Tokugawa Era (1603-1867), named for the Tokugawa clan which ruled Japan during this period. The latter part of the Era is characterized by highly sophisticated and refined aesthetics in arts, and great energy in popular culture. Mr. Tanikawa says that he was referring to the "sophisticated culture" of this Era.

Wasn't it Ooka Makoto[4] who said, "Mozart's daily life resided in music, not in his day-to-day living"? In other words, however hard you try to dig into Mozart's life, you will not find the secrets of his music. If you could write poetry in a different dimension, far removed from your own life, it would be wonderful, but that's not an easy thing to do. Somehow we can't shake off the dubious feeling that we write poetry to circumvent living. Or rather, poetry appears to be the product of such an effort. That is the difficulty that early modern to contemporary Japanese literature faces.

I am not saying that I know Tamura's day-to-day life, you see. All I know is a Tamura when he is drunk and happily manic, and a Tamura when he is sober and as meek as a borrowed cat. I don't know him in his depressive state, or while he is writing. But my mind conjures up his personality and his figure, you see, when I read lines such as the beginning of "The Perishable Substance:"

Soul is Form
If soul is form
what is it that's pale and trembling?

You see, these lines, in spite of myself, make me recall Tamura as he walked out of a porn movie house in San Francisco, saying that the close-up view of a vagina scared him. Also, take a look at the beginning lines of "The Study of Fear":

a single pin
drops to the floor, resounds
on an evening like this.

However I look at it, I think these lines originate from his own experience of a prolonged hangover. The sort of sensations that builds the foundation for his poetry not only exists in his poetry, but exists in his day-to-day living as well. In other words Tamura's

---

[4] Ooka Makoto is a contributor to this book. His bio can be found on page 89.

poetic diction originates from the convergence point of the two. This means each and every Tamura poem starts out from his actual sensations in life. If we were to describe the sensations in one word, it would be "fear."

—Yet, Mr. Tamura says, "Although I repeatedly talk about 'fear,' I don't have that fear in reality any more, you see . . . that fear exists in words."

That fear, the one that culminates in poetic diction, he may not have it any longer. But Tamura must have a lot of fear in real life. It seems to me that fear drives him to drink. When Tamura writes, he is trying to elevate fear of the mundane to the realm of poetry. I believe Tamura is so sensitive as to be fearful. Or rather he needs a fear that is both physiological and philosophical. Once he stops being fearful, he won't be Tamura anymore. He might end up being a retired old fellow next door. So it may be that while fear is driving him to drink, he is drinking to pursue it.

Even though he drinks heavily, I hear he is physically very healthy. When he stops drinking he doesn't seem to experience withdrawal, so I suppose he is not addicted. Tamura calls human kind the "Perishable Substance," but his words do not conjure some physical presence as Kaneko Mitsuharu's[5] words might. I wonder if that relates to the fact that he is essentially healthy and is from a family of great longevity. Tamura said, "When I talk about fear, its central axis is not a desire." I believe that is accurate. Tamura is free from avarice, I bet. Desires shape the reasons for our lives, so to be free from desires is tough, you know. The fact that he is free from desires makes him somewhat abstract, it seems to me. Feeling desirous heats a man up, but feeling fear chills him, you see. Tamura's words weave that sort of texture, which keeps me at a distance.

How should I say this? While Tamura has honed his insight to drill into the human condition, he shows little sympathy for or

---

[5] Kaneko Mitsuharu (1895-1975), poet.

rather interest in individuals per se. He tries to circumvent the area where human desires and enmities swirl. His favorite remark is, "That is a good person." But it seems to me that he is trying to force himself to be convinced of that, and to let himself look only at aspects of others that are relatively innocuous to him. Here again, that is because Tamura is fearful. He feels fear at each specific existence of an individual.

—Your thoughts on "Perishable Substance" and "The Study of Fear"?

Tamura's long poems have a certain characteristic tone, and in places they have beautiful and memorable lines. So, surprisingly, they are designed to intoxicate people. I personally have some resistance to being taken in by them. I prefer his shorter poems which are upbeat and witty. In terms of his story-telling, he uses casual Tokyo dialect with consummate skill. I have many examples of it that I love. Among them are "Obtuse Mind," "On My Way Home," and "Gods of Poetry."

I have heard Tamura read his own poems many times. He mumbles his poetry with no modulation. In contrast, I imagine he'd sing military songs with vigor, though I've never heard him sing them. The refined and memorable style of his long poems belongs to the print universe, not to the world of voice, I believe. If someone other than Tamura recites his piece, I would say the outcome would be the same. It is hard to explain, but that may be a symptom of the issues modern Japanese poetry faces. You see, it points to something deeper than Tamura's being shy in reading his own work out loud.

Tamura is not self-conscious about speaking of poetry or being a poet. He has absolutely no doubt about being a poet, yet the poetic voice he utters in the environment of day-to-day living is self-effacing. In his casual essays or in his dialogues with others when he is moderately fortified with alcohol, he is alive and well. So, as far as I am concerned, I would like to take in the totality of his linguistic activities, rather than to sanctify his poetry alone.

In this context, a presentation like the *Poetry and Criticism* series is superb. I don't know if Tamura invented the medium, but it is new as a genre, and fun to read. *A Poet's Notebook* also falls in that category. I understand some people regret the direction he is taking, but I think it's crafty of him to deal with aging or fermenting in that way. It could produce some good cheese, even though to some it may be light in flavor. Come to think of it, isn't there a cheese made from camel's milk, though I haven't yet tasted it?

(1977, *Leisurely Thoughts*)

[trans. Takako Lento]

TANIKAWA SHUNTARO (b. 1931) is the most widely read and highly acclaimed contemporary poet in Japan, and his work has been translated into many languages. Poet Murano Shiro wrote in 1968, "In terms of superb intelligence and sharp wit no modern [Japanese] poet can surpass him. One can see his work as the archetype of a new modern [Japanese] poetry to come after the poetry of the Arechi (Waste Land) group. " He was the first recipient of the Ayukawa Nobuo Award for poetry in 2010.

Tamura Ryuichi's Light Verse and the Poetry
of Everyday Life

Marianne Tarcov

Tamura Ryuichi's light poetry offers a rare avenue for this difficult, conceptual poet to address, in simple, ordinary language, the quirks and trivia of everyday life. Tamura's use of light verse as a mode for understanding the everyday is informed by the approach of his lifelong imaginative interlocutor, W.H. Auden, who, in a 1939 essay, defined light verse as the poetry of everyday life: "[p]oetry . . . having for its subject matter the everyday social life of its period or the experiences of the poet as an ordinary human being."[1] For Tamura Ryuichi, light verse offers sudden, often delightfully revelatory glimpses into ordinary human life that accessibly communicate their own brand of knowledge and understanding. Tamura's light poems reach for a mode of expression where all poetry becomes, in a sense, light, renouncing its alienated, oppositional cultural role for one of ordinary, everyday communication.

Tamura's light poetry of the everyday also fulfills a memorializing function. Two of Tamura's lighter poems featured in this volume, "Lieberman Goes Home" and "The Day the Mercury Sank,"

---

[1] From W. H. Auden's introduction to *The Oxford Book of Light Verse*, 1939.

are a kind of occasional verse: the poet writes in memory of a particularly important occasion in his life. These poems remain cheerfully confident in their own capacity to capture and memorialize the ephemeral, easily forgotten details of these moments. In his light work, Tamura offers a gentle, playful defense of poetry as an affirmative art, an art that offers a commemorative vehicle for trivial fragments of everyday experience that otherwise risk oblivion.

It is true that the darkness and difficulty of Tamura's best-known works—for example his debut collection *Four Thousand Days and Nights* [1956]—may seem to set them drastically apart from the light poems' clarity, simplicity, and sheer sense of fun. The light work's memorializing effort to capture otherwise lost aspects of human experience, however, is in a sense typical, even exemplary of Tamura's poetry. The speakers in Tamura's poems, light as well as serious, often serve as receptive instruments that gather the ephemera of human experience into a memorializing poetic structure.

Tamura's darker works betray a voracious receptivity to the lost fragments of human experience, especially to the traces of historical violence and loss underlying their postwar setting. For example, in the title work from Tamura's *Four Thousand Days and Nights*, the collective speaker "we" offers a series of self-injunctions to "[l]ook," "[l]isten," and "[r]emember" with all "our" strength for some elusive side of reality that remains imperceptible. The poem embodies a single desiring aspiration to see "what our eyes do not see," to hear "what our ears do not hear." Whether it is the changeable weather of "all the rainy cities," the delicate motion of "the trembling tongue of a single small bird," or "the tears of a single starved child," the "we" of "Four Thousand Days and Nights" finds unbearable the notion that any single fragment of human experience should end up relegated to oblivion or forgetfulness. In Tamura's light poems, these memorializing efforts aim, not at the traces of historical violence and loss preserved in the postwar "Four Thousand Days and Nights," but at the ephemeral substance of an everyday reality that has come to supersede or conceal them.

Lightness in Tamura's work often feels like a kind of substitute, a translucent facade that aspires to represent something else. The light poems describe themselves using the language of half-hidden secrets: "[T]here is a faint scent of / the secrets of creation and destruction of form," the speaker of "The Day The Mercury Sank" remarks, at once tremulously sensitive to this "faint scent" that pervades his daily reality, yet unable to satisfactorily render it. What is the elusive secret that permeates Tamura's light poems, and how does it effect its stealthy disruptions of its everyday setting?

The secret "faint scent" that underlies Tamura's light work frequently appears in terms of the weather, an ephemeral atmospheric reality whose often imperceptible shifts pervade ordinary human life. In both "Lieberman Goes Home" and "The Day the Mercury Sank," the poet's quirky sensitivity to even the subtlest fluctuations in weather becomes an ethically charged impulse to register and memorialize. Yet this very impulse remains premised on its own unrealizability, a horizon of representation that stays just out of each poem's reach. In Tamura's light verse, a poem serves as a barometric instrument whose function is to conscientiously record the scarcely perceptible, tiny eddies in the atmosphere of dailiness that invisibly surrounds it and render them perceptible in momentary flashes of intelligibility.

Lightness for Tamura serves as a vehicle for a surprising sense of sudden, delightful intelligibility, of disjunctive parts rendered momentarily into a still fragmentary but cohesive whole. For example, in the first stanza of "The Day The Mercury Sank," the rapid line breaks enact the same kind of fall into a new mode of understanding that they describe: "A deer at bay will fall from the cliff, / but for a human being to fall, / there has to be a poem." The line breaks in this stanza function at once as abrupt stops and as open-ended gestures of suturing and connection, creating a sense of disjunction that also feels connective. The stanza's final line, "there has to be a poem," feels as inevitable in light of its fragmentary predecessors as it does surprising. In this quintessential Tamura stanza, each one of its three fragmentary lineated components aspires to form a kind of interconnected whole. The "fall" precipitates the sudden, surprising moment when this sense of wholeness becomes intelligible. Yet the fall, and the moment of understanding it permits, is never final, unfolding instead as more and more poetry.

The formal procedures of these light poems enact their unrealizable aspiration to represent the ephemeral, weather-related phenomena that surround them. Formally, Tamura's light verse often mirrors the physical event of rainfall, in which ephemeral, transparent drops of water move downward through space, come to a sudden stop once they touch the ground, and repeat in a recursive structure. As seen in the stanza from "The Day the Mercury Sank" quoted above, Tamura's lineation in his light verse features fragmentary, crystalline linguistic units that move vertically through the white space of a page (Japanese is usually printed up-and-down) before they reach a sudden, often delightful stop that effortlessly opens up into its successor. The recursive "fall" into understanding that reoccurs at every line break remains forever incomplete, yet the failure of each "fall" provides the open-ended sense of possibility that its successor will succeed.

In his writing on humor, Tamura discusses the steep, surprising line breaks in his work in terms that recall the human being's fall that opens "The Day the Mercury Sank:"

> . . . I would like to write a poem in which the blanks that appear between each line become deep valleys. I wish I could successfully pull that off, but somehow I never manage to write quite that poem. Though it's actually when I don't try to write it that I end up getting beyond the words, I think. Yet, somehow it never quite gets there—I guess this is my idealism talking. When it comes to a good poem, I can see a deep valley in the space between each line and the next... I wish I could write the kind of poem that makes you wonder: will the reader just barely manage the leap, or, eyes closed, fall in halfway through and have to climb back up?[2]

The unrealizable poem Tamura can "never manage to write," in which each line break precipitates a readerly "fall" into a new mode of understanding, is a light one, rooted in a kind of comic sensibility that values speed and sudden reversals. Tamura posits his unrealizable fall as a motive that provides the impulse for his poetic work,

---

[2] Tamura Ryuichi, "Kyofu Fuan Yumoa," *Gendaishi Yomihon Tamura Ryuichi* (Tokyo: Shichosa, 2000): 313.

a desire horizon that keeps receding and so animates the act of writing. In this passage, the act of writing appears as a recursively repeating, perpetually incomplete fall through "the space between each line and the next." Light verse, and the sudden yet repeated fall into intelligibility it offers, is not a separate genre of literary expression for Tamura. It is a horizon to which all his work aspires.

Tamura's light "fall" into a new mode of understanding owes much to the material slipperiness of poetic language, its hapless penchant to fall just short of its unrealizable aspiration to offer a linguistic representation of reality. In the light poem "Lieberman Goes Home," the poem's fall into a gap between poetic language and the often dispiritingly commercial reality it seeks to represent becomes an opportunity ripe for slapstick pratfalls. Puns in "Lieberman Goes Home" render a quintessential poetic dilemma comic, playfully exploring a poetic rift between words and their referents without pretending to bridge it. This poem rejoices in the inexhaustible gap between language and what it seeks to represent, playfully oscillating back and forth from confusion to momentary flashes of intelligibility.

"Lieberman Goes Home" commemorates a fairly ordinary occasion in the poet's life, a farewell party for a visiting American poet, Laurence Lieberman. The poem portrays Lieberman as a "rainy day man," a common Japanese expression for a man who encounters rainy weather wherever he goes. In the course of the poem, however, the particular character of the "rainy day man" becomes a weather-related figure for poets in general, haplessly struggling to linguistically represent the stormy atmosphere that surrounds them, threatening to overwhelm them at any moment. The rainy day man has a ludicrously intense sensitivity to the fluctuations in weather that permeate the poem, as well as a tendency to parody them in verse. In this poem, the vertiginous falls of Tamura's lineation take on a parodic dimension, mirroring the ups and downs of the systems of commerce and exchange that surround them with meaningfully comic flair: "When the yen was revaluated, the dollar dropped. The rainy day man dropped to his knees and wept. / Our rainy day man is a poet, so he wrote a poem for *The New Yorker*: 'The Dollar's Lament.'" The poetic line breaks to mirror the drop of the dollar-yen exchange rate. Poetry as falling tears parodies commerce as rainfall, with the poet as rainy day man using one to poetically approximate the other as best he can.

The "rainy day man's" propensity to parody the pervasive commercial structures that surround him comes uncomfortably close to reproducing them. The "rainy day man's" capacity to indiscriminately register and memorialize the atmosphere around him does not include an ability to reliably edit or make judgments. "Lieberman Goes Home" cites pervasive tropes of sexism and nationalist sentiment in a manner that leaves the poet's attitude toward these tropes troublingly unclear. The speaker refers in a possibly dismissive tone to "some woman's lib professor" who, he believes, is out to steal his friend's university position, and jokingly refers to the wife of his American friend as a "polar bear," suggesting he sees her as huge, white, and nonhuman. Later in the poem, the speaker cites Japanese anti-American sentiment in a manner that could be said to trivialize legitimate leftist Japanese anger at American policies: "*But in Japan we've got a bunch of / petty progressive peasants. When it comes to America, all they can do / is keep talking about the Viet Nam War and racism.*" In his drunken, uninhibited state, the poet adopts a pose of oblivious distance from the social and political workings of the real world, blithely ignoring the troubling implications of his comments.

The poet as hapless "rainy day man" may possess ludicrously intense insight into the workings of weather, but this insight brings home what the poem sees as its own inability to penetrate the workings of the other big systems that permeate its world: commerce, transnational exchange, racism, sexism, and politics. The poem absurdly posits the weather as a zero-sum system of exchange, in which the rainy day man actually risks running out of the rainfall that provides the animating motive for his work: "*It doesn't rain very much in Illinois, / so get as wet as you can in the rainy season of Japan. / Oh! Get those big blue eyes wet:* our manic-depressive Lieberman is going home." The poet's lugubrious eyes reflect the rain of the season as it changes. The poet remains vulnerable to changeable systems of weather—seasonal, psychic, and especially linguistic—and very much confused about how they work. The "rainy day man" mistakenly posits the weather as a zero-sum game, when in fact the unrealizable, infinitely recursive quality of his poetic enterprise renders the weather inexhaustible. The poet as "rainy day man" remains sheepishly aware of the limited, narrow quality of his perspective, and he does not pretend to know everything, or even to know much of anything at all. "I'm so drunk, I don't know what I'm talking about," the speaker admits toward the end of the poem. There remains a sense of optimistic, unrealized possibility in the undetermined realm of what the poet does not yet know.

The poem knows more than the "rainy day man" who inhabits it. For a moment, the speaker glimpses this infinitely receding horizon of understanding. At one point, the speaker, carried away with the oddly beautiful "wobbling" motion of the mosquito larvae that seasonally signify spring in Kamakura, begins to bodily "wobble" himself, unsteadily attempting to stand upright after too much whisky. Indeed, it is the whole poem that wobbles precariously, cheerfully disoriented by its self-generated whirlwind of changing, shifting meanings:

> Kamakura is just about starting the rainy season,
> and while the pond may not be quite as big as Lake
>   Michigan, it is infested with
> wobbling mosquito larvae.
> So up I wobble to my feet
> whisky tipsy,
> and make a speech.

The onomatopoetically doubled Japanese word for wobble, *hyoro-hyoro*, contains a repetition within itself, which Tamura intensifies by repeating the word. The repeated whisper of *hyoro-hyoro* bridges the unmanageable gap between the long, overstuffed line containing the first "wobble" and the tiny fragment that holds the second. The poet registers the quiet flicker of the *hyoro-hyoro* springtime wobbling in the air, and reproduces it with his own trembling body.

The poem's precarious wobbling precipitates a fall. This moment in the poem opens into a montage-like juxtaposition between Kamakura and Lake Michigan. The playful repetition-within-a-repetition of the two *hyoro-hyoros* ushers in a moment of spatial expansiveness. Kamakura and Lake Michigan overlap for a moment of drunkenly altered perception, placed in proximity as uncomfortable as it is absurd in light of the speaker's provocative political comments.

In "Lieberman Goes Home," Tamura's formal procedures become most fully realized when they relinquish their hold on the poem they purport to unify. The poem's playful linguistic procedures eventually end in a rigorously self-effacing valedictory gesture, then trail off into nothing at all. "Lieberman Goes Home" ends with a series of bilingually punning goodbyes: "See you later, hippo hipster! *Arigato*, alligator!" (a play on *aba yo, kaba yo* [Japanese for "Bye, hippo"], the common American expression "See you later, alligator," and the Japanese *arigato*), cheerfully laughing itself out of existence. The poem's closing act of relinquishment takes on a ghostly quality, as it ends with a human voice saying goodbye.

The rainy day man's mission—intelligibility through poetic play—finally becomes a memorial or valedictory one. The poem's repeated, increasingly incoherent efforts to end itself suggest that it still has more to say, that there will always be more to say. Our last glimpse of the rainy day man, abstracted in (drunken) reverie, suggests that the poem's ending lapses into the kind of generative though perhaps socially awkward silence that waits tensely for someone to break it: "Only our rainy day man is staring into space, staring. Into space." In "Lieberman Goes Home," the act of closure feels elliptical rather than final, and there remains room for our hapless rainy day man to keep trying his hand at the inexhaustible linguistic rift that continually trips him up.

In the other light poem contained in this volume, "The Day the Mercury Sank," which describes Tamura's 1973 meeting with W. H. Auden in New York, the poet once again undertakes the rainy day man's quixotic mission. This time, our rainy day man has a barometric sensitivity to dips in temperature or atmospheric pressure. In this poem, the poet as barometric instrument gently undertakes a memorializing mission: to register the tiny, almost imperceptible shifts in the weathery atmosphere and record them. The poem serves as a potentially redemptive historical instrument that revives and memorializes fragments of ordinary human experience that would otherwise stay lost.

Like "Lieberman Goes Home," "The Day the Mercury Sank" hinges on confusion followed by a moment of sudden, lighthearted understanding. In Auden's apartment, the speaker acknowledges his desire to bring some kind of "secret to light." He searches the room for traces of something he cannot quite perceive, looking for an unknowable "secret" in the clutter of the apartment. The speaker cannot resist enumerating the flotsam and jetsam in the room—"a typewriter and scattered sheets of music," "strong coffee, a dry martini, and a pack of Lucky Strike," the pictures on the walls—and invests these random objects with poignant aliveness. The clutter gives nothing away: the speaker notes that, unlike the clutter of a painter's studio, a poet's clutter reveals little about his personality or creative process.

Yet in their very reticence, the fragments of the poet's life that fill the tiny space of his urban apartment reveal as much as they obscure: "A portrait of E. M. Forster / and a watercolor of an Austrian mountain villa: / enough to bring this poet's secret to light." The poem collects and captions the objects that surround it, integrating the typewriter, musical scores, coffee, liquor, cigarettes, and hanging pictures into a poetic inventory that the speaker eventually finds revelatory. The onset of sudden intelligibility happens at the very moment the speaker admits himself baffled by the awkwardness of the cross-cultural interaction between himself and his interlocutor, unable to "keep up with poet's English."

Suddenly, as the speaker examines the pictures on the walls, Auden's little room veers from cozy familiarity to vertiginous expansiveness. For what happens to the weather inside a small, contained interior space like Auden's small New York apartment? The weather expands and enlarges the interior space that aspires to hold it, like a gaseous substance that takes the shape of its container. The poem has so much trouble containing its own contents that it oscillates between closed and open-ended stanzas, that is, between stanzas that enjamb and stanzas that contain a whole sentence bounded by an end stop. As the poem proceeds, the neatly closed stanzas of the opening give way to open-ended stanzas that end mid-sentence and continue across a gulf of white space:

Of course, there's nothing novel about a poet's workroom.
In a painter or sculptor's atelier,
there is a faint scent of

the secrets of creation and destruction of form.
What we had here was strong coffee, a dry martini,
    and a pack of Lucky Strike.
I couldn't quite keep up with poet's English,

so I just looked at the wall. A portrait of E. M. Forster
and a watercolor of an Austrian mountain villa:
enough to bring this poet's secret to light.
The "individual" who acknowledged himself heir to
    Victorian culture, Austrian forest,
and New York backstreets.

The speaker's glance at the pictures on the wall has the dizzying effect of bringing the outside world inside the room. The poem opens itself up to the pictures' scenes of Auden's life, and the speaker finds himself wandering through them. "I was in 'In Time of War,'" the speaker marvels, citing a 1939 Auden poem as if he has come to bodily inhabit the text the same way he has Auden's room. The speaker rests inside the cozily closed yet suddenly expansive poetic room, enjoying a momentary sense that he has brought to light the secret he was looking for. The poem becomes an interior room of its own that gathers the fragments of everyday human life into a memorial structure and protectively shelters them for as long as it can.

The space of Auden's room has opened itself up to reveal the lived experience that underlies yet perpetually eludes poetry. When light poems do manage to precipitate their sudden, delightful "fall" into intelligibility, it is by means of the experiential lens of the everyday, which does not always quite match up with the conceptual framework of poetic language. "The Day the Mercury Sank" ends, like "Lieberman Goes Home," with a gentle valedictory gesture that dissipates the ephemeral constellation of intelligibility it has generated: "The poet's great hand shook mine in farewell." Yet the poem manages to pull off a farewell gesture that does not quite feel final. The "secret" the speaker hoped to find in the scattered everyday detritus of the room revealed itself for a moment, but has now returned to its obscurity, leaving the two poets unable to verbally communicate their shared experience. The mysterious gap between human experience and poetic language's capacity to render it intelligible reopens, rendered somehow different by the speaker's meaningful encounter with another human being. "There has to be a poem," in the words of the opening stanza of "The Day the Mercury Sank," because each time a poem momentarily inhabits the gap that separates language from human experience, it brings the two together into a new and potentially transformative configuration.

Tamura's faith in the transformative potential of light verse in poems recalls Auden's 1939 description of lightness as a leftist-inflected imaginative act of world-building. Auden sees light verse as an attempt to imagine a society where all poetry is "simple, clear, and gay" because it belongs to ordinary people, rather than to poets as an isolated class:

> In such a society, and in such alone, will it be possible for the poet, without sacrificing any of his subtleties of sensibility or his integrity, to write poetry which is simple, clear, and gay...For poetry which is at the same time light and adult can only be written in a society which is both integrated and free.[3]

Auden suggests that light verse partakes of an unrealized social order where poetic expression occurs unhindered by political and social inequalities. When it comes to Auden's vision of lightness, the poet speaks not for himself alone, but for a collective entity of ordinary people.

Read beside Auden's vision of light verse as a utopian poetic act aimed at "a society which is both integrated and free," Tamura's light work tempt us to read him as a profoundly optimistic poet, one who genuinely believes in the necessity of each single poem's "fall" into a differently imagined world. Tamura's light poems are at heart transformative, as his reflection on humor's capacity to transform the way people relate to the world and to each other suggests:

---

[3] Again, from Auden's introduction to *The Oxford Book of Light Verse*.

[W]hen this kind of humor isn't there, a certain kind of human sensibility can't come to be. The capacity to change sides, that's what a sense of humor really is, isn't it? To transform one's point of view, not to look at things in just one way. And the precise way in which that change in point of view happens can open up our capacity for receptivity. The world as it is ends in, if I dare to use this word, the word "tragedy," but even this "tragedy" has more than one side to it.[4]

Tamura's light work shares with his more serious poetry an aspiration towards a potentially redemptive perceptual transformation wrought on an otherwise bleak reality. The difference lies in the light poems' emphasis on "a certain kind of human sensibility," a world of comically fraught interpersonal encounters and everyday communication. For Tamura, the tragedy of the real world has an elusive other side, and lightness has the potential to represent this other side in sudden flashes of comic understanding. Tamura's light verse reveals that while "the world as it is" may present itself as a reality that has already hardened into inevitability, it actually remains a playfully precarious contingency vulnerable to transformation, however momentary, effected by artful maneuvers in human perception. Through its playful linguistic "falls," Tamura's light verse embodies an unrealized world where all poetry is everyday, and the everyday has turned into poetry.

(2010)

[translations by Tarcov unless otherwise noted]

MARIANNE TARCOV is currently working toward a PhD in Japanese Literature at the University of California, Berkeley, where her focus is 20th century Japanese poetry. She spent 2006-7 as a Fulbright Fellow at Kanto Gakuin University in Yokohama, Japan. Her translations have apperaed in *Poetry Kanto*, *Kyoto Journal*, and elsewhere.

---

[4] Tamura 312.

Sparks from Tamura's Smithy

Laurence Lieberman

In my first eleven years of teaching, I'd never been awarded any released-time. Sabbatical leaves were no possible option at the College of the Virgin Islands, where I was hired to launch the first English Department of the fledgling school in St. Thomas. Then, during my third year at the University of Illinois, I was surprised to be granted a full-year leave to travel to Japan and write a portfolio of poems about my experiences abroad.

In choosing Japan, I was following a childhood dream prompted by a cousin I idolized—fifteen years my senior—who spent a couple of years in Japan as a military serviceman with the occupation forces, just after the end of World War II. In our long chain of letters he told me marvelous haunting stories about Japanese survivor-families, and he sent me an odd assortment of memorabilia—medals, ribbons, coins, and finally, both a bayonet from a rifle that clearly had seen action and a metal helmet sporting one bullet hole. And he'd also somehow come into possession of a rare original manuscript of Lafcadio Hearn's writings. I never saw the much-touted scroll of parchment, but I was privy to many intriguing details of his getting the literary treasure authenticated. Its estimated value kept soaring, from month to month. He kept the wrinkled pages hidden away in his leather knapsack as he traveled, and he confided to me that he stored them in an old footlocker with mothballs when he returned home the following year. My child ears were bewitched by the fairytale overtones of his eventual plans to have the secret scroll published.

*

My wife and I decided to travel to Japan by ship for the pleasures of a sea voyage, and to ease our children's shock of transition to a totally unfamiliar culture. En route, we became friends with Marilia Corbot, a young Brazilian woman who was planning to marry a Japanese poet—Yoshimasu Gozo—soon after her arrival in Tokyo. She and Gozo had met in Iowa City the previous year, where they both had attended the international program for writers. Marilia generously invited us to her wedding. We had arranged to live in Tokyo for our first few weeks, since a colleague of mine from University of Illinois had just vacated an apartment in Shinjuku, and we conveniently picked up the last month of his lease.

Marilia's wedding was a lavish celebration. It was a lucky chance for us to make friends and become acquainted with many Japanese customs and rituals. After the wedding, Gozo promptly introduced us to his literary friends, Tamura Ryuichi and Niikura Toshikazu. It was clear from the tone of Gozo's tribute to Tamura that not only did he greatly admire the elder poet, but he regarded him as his special mentor as well. We hadn't received any advance word about Tamura before the wedding day, contrary to his own joking speculation that Marilia had warned us on shipboard about her fiancé's old drinking buddy—as Tamura reports in his charming little essay about our friendship:

> Many different topics must have come up during the long journey . . . "A drinking friend of Yoshimasu's, an old man who writes poetry himself, is living in Kamakura." "We want to live in Kamakura. Please introduce this old man to us." "But this old poet, he's very much a drunk." Such words were undoubtedly exchanged.

Both of these poets had been awarded grants to the prestigious Iowa program. Evidently, much of Gozo's fellowship time in Iowa City was concurrent with Tamura's second visit, and they'd grown very close during that time.

Our family still had a couple of weeks left on our Tokyo apartment's lease. We hadn't made any plans yet for moving to our next home, but we knew that we preferred to rent a true Japanese house, sleep on futon mats on tatami floors, and hopefully, send our children—ages seven to eleven—to a Japanese school. Soon after we met, Tamura suggested that we consider looking for a home in Kamakura, and we were extremely touched by his offer to shepherd us. His description of his family's life in that historic town made it sound most attractive. Within a few days, we visited the lovely seaside village of Yuigihama and quickly found a Kamakura house to our liking with the help of Tamura's then-wife and Niikura Toshikazu, who had studied at U.S. universities and facilitated exchanges between prospective landlords and ourselves. As Tamura points out in his essay, his wife had to strongly argue on our behalf to overcome the homeowner's initial reluctance to rent to a foreign family. A week later, we happily moved our light baggage from Tokyo to Kamakura.

*

Shortly after the wedding, Tamura, Niikura, and I had fleetingly spoken about the prospect of my translating some of Tamura's poetry into English during my time in Japan. Niikura's proficiency in both languages would compensate for my very weak Japanese. A professor of American Literature at Meiji Gakuin University, he felt confident that he'd be able to mediate between us, providing nominal versions of the poems in lusterless English which I hoped to refashion into verses that might both capture the spirit of the original texts and become vivid and readable English poems in their own right.

I'd never done any translating before, but for some time I had felt that if the right occasion came along, I would love to have a chance to learn the craft. Tamura and I seemed to feel an instant rapport, and we quickly developed an affinity for the recent poems we shared with one another, despite some radically opposite stylistic leanings. In particular, his poetic language was spare and the hard cutting edge of his measure was austere, or so I supposed, whereas I was given to sensory elaboration and expansive meters. To be sure, we were an odd couple, and it was quite a challenge for me to learn to curb my excesses. Professor Niikura, who is a truly gifted teacher, did a remarkable job of guiding me to find a diction and voice that might complement Tamura's uniquely natural delivery. Only following many revisions, fine-tuned by sensitive feedback from Niikura, did I seem to strike the right balance.

If Tamura's subject or thesis struck a familiar chord with me, it helped me to close the gap between our sensibilities. "The Beacon Light of Oshima" is surely one of my better efforts, no doubt helped by my personal identification with the lighthouse itself, since my house on Yuigihama beach faced the revolving beacon light, and its eerie presence fluttered across my frequent walks at daybreak and twilight:

THE BEACON LIGHT OF OSHIMA

I hate a new house.
Maybe because
I was
Born and brought up in an old house.

There is neither a table to dine with the dead,
Nor minute slits or grooves
For organic burrowers
To inhabit. "The pear tree is split," I wrote in my poem

Twenty years ago or so.
I have planted another pear tree
In the diminutive soil of my garden.
In the morning, I sprinkle water over it.

I wish I could grow death inside the new pear tree.
I wish it could drink itself to death

Out of my hand, living out
Its own green dying.

I wish we could bloom slowly into our own green death.
I wish all day.
At night I read Victorian pornography.
I tell myself I have no illusion about the future.

That is my only illusion. That I have none. Or,
That we have any future. . . .
There goes that flash above the horizon forty kilometers
Out to sea

From my study window:
The beacon light of Oshima
Island. Thirty years old or so.
Every thirteen minutes, it squelches my thought.

I grew to love this poem's gentle touch and quiet humor. Several of the artist's recurrent motifs come into play here, his great ardor for non-human forms of life—plants and animals alike—and his conviction that it is ennobling for us to pull away from the artifacts of human civilization, then draw closer to our fellows of the parallel worlds of flora and fauna: "I wish we could bloom slowly into our own green death."

I enjoyed an even stronger spirit of kinship with Tamura's pair of poems recounting his auspicious meeting with W. H. Auden in New York City. I, too, had met Auden a couple years earlier in Riverside, California, following a brilliant reading of his poetry. No more than four or five of us were treated to a winning high-spirited chat with him for nearly an hour. We sat in a circle drooped on easy chairs of a small drawing room. His answers to our questions were forthright and loquacious, and he seemed utterly without pretense. From time to time, his hand swept back the thick swatch of brown hair that crept over his forehead wrinkles. His laughter was infectious, and he often reduced us to happy titters. When I read Auden's poems today, I usually recall this lively occasion.

In conversations with my new friends, I was pleased to hear that Auden and John Berryman were among the few American poets most admired by young Japanese authors. I had recently written review-essays of their latest books for my regular column in *The Yale Review*. (And the year before we moved to Japan, I had hosted Berryman for a visit of several days in Urbana; then, shortly after his shocking death, I was commissioned to write a memorial piece about him for the Japanese journal *Eigo Seinen* [*The Rising Generation*], which appeared in May 1972.) Our mutual fondness for these authors provided common ground for many of my talks with Tamura and Niikura, and it helped to foster a trust between us. My own serious reading in current Japanese literature was more addressed to fiction writers than poets—Kawabata and Mishima, especially. The more we conversed about authors whose works we all admired, the more it enhanced our three-way work process. Early on, Niikura informed me that his favorite teacher at Princeton University had been my good friend the poet Ted Weiss. No wonder, I reflected, Niikura went on to become such a discerning teacher himself.

*

For me, the most exhilarating challenge of our collaboration was our work with Tamura's two-poem sequence about W. H. Auden. The first poem—"The Day the Mercury Sank"—memorializing Tamura's encounter with the Anglo-American in his flat in Manhattan, is included in the front pages of this book. Marianne Tarcov's expert translation rings true to both the spirit and letter of the original verses. The expanded version of this poem that I finally produced runs to more than twice the length of this piece.

Tamura and I found ourselves reminiscing, at some length, about each of our encounters with Auden, and we also discussed our mutual love for his poetry. I had already completed a number of translations of a more conventional kind, such as "The Beacon Light of Oshima," and the Auden sequence roused me to want to experiment with a freer approach to reinventing the original works. Certainly, I was fascinated with Tamura's art of condensing the rich adventure of his memorable visit into so few telling details; and indeed, I came away from his poem feeling that he has amazingly given us the whole story, since the poignant, terse images that he presents have a magical resonance that sweeps beyond the literal events and give the reader the exact tone of that time and place. Tamura benefits from his sharp journalist's eye for selecting the few items that inescapably capture—and indeed, galvanize—the feel, the taste, the whiff, the total *nuance* of the setting.

With no disrespect, then, for the strength of the original poem, I set out to model my new version of the work largely after Robert Lowell's avowed esthetic in his book *Imitations*: "I have been reckless with literal meaning and labored hard to get the tone . . . I have tried to write alive English and to do what my authors might have done if they were writing their poems now in America . . . I have tried to keep something equivalent to the fire and finish of my originals." Nonetheless, I suspect that I have asserted still more freedom from the original texts, even, than Lowell condones in his groundbreaking book of translations. During my year in Japan, I was much steeped in reading Lowell's recent poetry, the early cycles of his *Notebook* in particular, not just the translations. And I was also taking a cue from other poet-translators I emulated—James Wright, Mark Strand, Stephen Berg.

I subtitle the Auden poems "Improvisations on a Theme from the Japanese of Ryuichi Tamura," to take account of the wide leeway I gave myself. My talks with Tamura about his Auden poems came to resemble—more than ever before—interviews with the author, in which I was searching for the primal roots of the experience he drew upon during the act of composition. I believe that I was able to convey to him and Niikura that my plan—for once—was to expand his poems into a hybrid work that would allow me to re-envisage the happenings on the page as if viewed through my own eyes, or as if recycled through my nervous system. Perhaps to one degree or another, most translators find they are trying to foster in themselves the illusion of becoming the other author, slipping in and out of his skin as if his epidermal shell were a form of garb that could be transferred from one soul to another. But in my case, there was a more deliberate attempt to go back to the core events and scene that had inspired the poem, inviting the author to revisit that setting with me in the interview, then scouting around for other raw materials that might have been kept in—rather than excluded—

by his refining art. In our talk, we were playing with parallels between us: my first-hand take on Auden could be appended to his in the hybrid version, his memory of residing in Iowa the year before somehow grafted onto my current visit to Japan . . .

But as I revised the work, I felt that the most important new dimension was my trance of becoming an invisible third party who was privileged to attend that setting, a secret sharer of the room beside the two master poets. Hence, my prospective reader would view both Tamura and Auden through my eyes, as well as Tamura's. We find some elements of a self-portrait in Tamura's short poem, but my new version amplifies the portrayals of Tamura and Auden to include traits of their person that I found to be most starkly memorable—in particular, their ears and their hands:

> The day when the mercury
>   sank, I rose
>   with the twilight moon
>   of twenty below zero, climbing
>
>   two rickety flights of steps to visit the evening star
>   of Western poets. The Anglo-American Fuji!
>   In the East Village, New York,
>   I mounted the summit
>
>   to his upstairs back alley cold water flat slowly enough
>   to help the rising full moon to help
>   nameless tottering city skeletons
>   unbending to lift
>
>   thousands of shovelfuls of three-foot-deep
>   all day's falling moon
>   snow, sending back fullmoonfall . . .
>   Two flat boards backed
>
>   the cracked pane. Here, too—*eminence perched*
>   *on squalor!* I mused, as my footfalls
> grew fainter and fainter dimmed by my pulse's thudding
>   in my pixy-erect ears buried

in vapor blooms of panted breathsteam
exhaled between gulps of the dank thin upperair ether
  above the timber line of the tallest
  lamppost . . . *A deer at bay falls from the cliff* . . .

  Abruptly, the door swung open.
  Back from my raised hand.
  My sharp knuckles poised to rap. Left hanging
    In naked blunder.

  Nowhere to hide. No way
to shelter the frail exposed sparrows' wings
  of my open palms: the long slender
plumes of my tapering fingers grew slimmer, narrowed:

I saw as if for the first time their much-touted platform
  scrawniness, as they rose and fell,
    dwarfed and swaddled in the voluminous pumping
    handclasp of my host—

    palms lumpish,
    knuckles swollen like walnuts.
    And it may be I reddened
  to the sharp-cornered tips of my high elfin ears

as I stared at the thick puffy barnacles, pendulous,
    drooping over his sideburns.
  I scanned the poet's room, blank
    and bare and square.

    A small low stool.
    A typewriter on the desk.
A few sheets of a musical score dropped at random—
no surprise to me! A poet's workroom

    may hide the stains of his craft . . .[1]

_____

[1] Excerpted from *Two for the Evening Star.*

The unseen third pair of eyes in the room adds another layer of observation to the dramatic brief encounter of the two sovereign artists. Tamura's first-person voice is still the conduit of images throughout, but a pale guest of history—intrusive or not—enlarges the scale of the panorama. In Lowell's phrase, I wished to have found a new "equivalent to the fire and finish" of Tamura's original vision. I like to think my expanded sketch of improvisations will add helpful elements for American readers coming to Tamura's work for the first time.

My version of the second poem in the Auden sequence, "Portrait of the Poet," is a sweeping full-blown litany of images. Tamura and I had both been deeply moved by a recent photograph of Auden—honoring his sixty-fifth birthday—on the cover of *The Atlantic Monthly*. Again, I invited Tamura to share with me any helpful ideas or hints about his pick of images that aspired to form—as he proposed—a map-like composite of Auden's magisterially weathered-looking face in the tableaux of his poem. From line to line, he spontaneously rattled off a chain of free associations sparked anew by each image, and I took ample notes, eager to save these extra resources to fortify the range of details I might draw on to devise my hybrid translation. As it happens, this was the last poem of Tamura's that I struggled to plot out before I left Japan and returned home. Again, my plan was to pore over this interview material and recover some remnants of Tamura's own smithy, his creation forge, to shape my version of his litany of images . . . But shortly after my arrival in Urbana, I checked my mail and discovered—to my surprise—that Auden's agent had just written to me the week before to inform me of Auden's availability to give a public reading in the visiting writers program I hosted for the University of Illinois. I happily arranged to set the date for an Auden appearance on our campus in early Fall, and I began firing off flyers to promote the upcoming event to all relevant media.

In early spring of that year, Auden had "returned to Oxford." His agent informed me: "He now resides at Christ Church College, where he is an honorary student, but he retains his U.S. citizenship." Less than two weeks prior to his scheduled visit to Urbana, we received the grievous news of his sudden death from a heart attack. I had kept several engrossing photos of Auden that were sent to me by his book publisher and his agent, each a pose distinct from the others. Never any least attempt to conceal the many wrinkles or blotches of his aging. The new pix added their luminous glimmerings to my copy of *The Atlantic Monthly* cover photo. I have kept them all in plain view on my office walls ever since, and I communed with the pictures, of course, as I completed my last version of a Tamura poem:

PORTRAIT OF THE POET

Today I saw the magazine cover picture of your sixty-fifth-birthday face.
    In the deep fissures of your brow, I traced a map of wars:

canyon-floors flecked with the hoofprints of advancing cavalries,
    the bootprints of stamping infantries;

and in the ravines of your cheeks, more lightly pocked, I deciphered
    the hands-and-knees' prints of trapped and fleeing innocents;

and in those wide crevasses, quartermoon-curves, under your eyes,
    I decoded permanent faults left by facial earthquakes,

the three or four continental shelves of your lower face slipping and sliding
    against each other, violently grinding their surfaces,

as each fracture in the political earth's crust—each world conflagration—
    left its imprint in the gulleys of your jaws, the cleft of your chin.

In all those haunted grooves, chiseled and gouged from left to right,
    I read blueprints of history—yours and ours—

    as in the fork-tipped veinwork of leaf-fossils

    as in the creases in a torn-out page of biblical scripture
      folded and unfolded for thousands of rereadings,
    hidden by day in the underclothes of the atheist's slave

as in the many-layered cross-section of the crumpled wall
    of a twelfth-century brickwork shrine, war-ravened
survivor of twice-a-dozen remortarings and replasterings

as in stitching and unstitching of immortal lines in a score
    of manuscript revisions of Yeats's "Sailing to Byzantium"

as in the workmanlike beveled edges and keenly trained rhymes
    of your own immortalizing verses to Yeats

as in the strata and substrata of mineral veins, sedimentary
    lodes deposited by ancient underground streams
long since run dry, and now embedded in layered sheets of the rock,
    charting, stratum by mineral-rich stratum,
the great ages of geologic time

as in scorched and blackened streaks in the bark of the charred
    center-beam timbers of a reconstructed Buddhist temple
bombed-out and incinerated by B-52s in World War II,
    counter-flames from the unkilled cedar-trunks burning outward
from their life-cores, standing off the flames of TNT

So must your inner-life burning withstand war's omnivorous fire-storms.
So bespeaks the burnt-cork-stained wide trenches of your face.

*

The shock of Auden's dying just before his autumn trip to Illinois
resonated—to my bewilderment—with several other recent deaths of
great writers during my spring months in Kamakura. Knowing my af-
fection for the novels of Kawabata, Tamura generously arranged an ap-
pointment for me to meet his much-revered friend at Kawabata's
apartment in a highrise tower just a few miles up the coast from Yuigi-
hama. As I recall, this apartment complex at Zushi Point was much the
tallest building in the Province.

    Lately, there was a considerable amount of talk among writers
about Mishima's fairly recent ritual suicide. I myself had been coping

with bouts of depression, intermittently, since mid-winter, and the news of John Berryman's suicidal leap from the bridge in Minneapolis one week before my planned date with Kawabata surely added to my gloom. When my dark mood partially lifted, I kept plugging away at revisions of my longest poem, "The Osprey Suicides," in response to many helpful suggestions from editor Howard Moss in his guardedly encouraging letter offering to reconsider a new version of my manuscript for *The New Yorker*. (That's the work of mine Tamura refers to in his comical poem, "Lieberman Goes Home." Clearly, though I don't remember it now, I must have used the proceeds of the check to pay for everyone's dinner at the "fine restaurant.")

How well I remember that the last week before I was scheduled to meet Kawabata was my most despondent time. On Thursday, two days before my appointment three miles up the beach, my awful mood bottomed out and suddenly vanished as I ran down the shore behind my American friend's house. The next morning, I received a phone call from Tamura. His voice was trembling as he told me that Kawabata had died the night before—he had gassed himself in his apartment.

On a cheerier note, my family's last months in Kamakura were among the happiest. Whenever we visited the Tamura household, my daughters loved to watch Mrs. Tamura feed her little birds from the tip of her tongue. Most mornings, my son Isaac and I trotted over to the fish market nearest our house to get an early pick of the fresh sliced tuna, yellowtail, and salmon—we were still addicted to sashimi when others in our family had grown tired of that cuisine.

Toward the last days, we sought every opportunity to spend extra time with our friends. The most frequent visitor to our home was a young Japanese man from Hokkaido whom we had met on shipboard, Toshi Arisaka. We'd shared quarters with him in a lower berth of our ship's hold on the way to Japan from California. The children loved their bunk beds and became fast friends with Toshi before my wife and I fully made his acquaintance. Toshi had completed his masters degree at San Francisco State University just a few weeks before the voyage, and he was returning to Tokyo to begin his career as a translator. He was one of that special breed of cripples who makes you forget almost immediately after you first encounter him that he has any handicap at all. Childhood polio had left him with one foot all gnarled and twisted to one side, but he laughed at any mention of his deformity, and soon he had us all chuckling with him. He treated his crutches like toys when he played with the children. He was very short of stature—about the same height as eleven-year-old Carla—but his bright spirit lifted him beyond measure. He was to become quite the world traveler and often visited us in America over the next ten years, or so. Then we lost touch.

On the day of our departure from Japan, Toshi was in the forefront of the entourage of sweet friends who accompanied us to our ship at the Yokohama dock. "Two Songs of Leave-taking" is my recapitulation of the events reported in Tamura's bon voyage poem for my family, "Lieberman Goes Home." Likewise, the following excerpt is my chant of thanks for the prodigal gifts we'd received all year from our Japanese friends:

> Toshi is waving his crutch
> high—oh, high!—over all heads, needling through
> the spaghetti
>   webwork of streamers. Now Mrs. Tamura
>   has leapt upon Mr.
>   Tamura's back, and both
>   are waving to us—
>
>   to the lost United
> States buried in us—waving with that circular
> spinning motion,
>   the hand call to meet again, meet again,
>   oh, anyplace on earth!
>
>   . . . But song
> in my ears at the last is dear Mr. Niikura's
> telephone

blessings our final two days: "Phone me, or I
  you, for anything, nothing,
  today, tomorrow, today,
    again and again . . ."

(2010)

LAURENCE LIEBERMAN has published fourteen books of poetry and three
books of criticism. Recent books include *Carib's Leap: Selected & New Poems
of the Caribbean* (Peepal Tree, 2005; UK), *The Regata in the Skies: Selected Long
Poems* (UGA Press, 1999), and *Beyond the Muse of Memory: Essays on Contem-
porary American Poets* (U of Missouri Press, 1995). He was the founding ed-
itor of the Illinois Poetry Series (1971-2009) and is Professor Emeritus of
English at University of Illinois.

Exceptional Poet: Tamura Ryuichi

Yoshimasu Gozo

Tamura Ryuichi, this exceptional poet. . . . As I wrote the word "exceptional" in two ideograms, 例 (example)外 (outside), I felt as if these ideograms are images hanging loose somewhere like in a window, or an opening of my retina. So even though I knew I needed to finish this article in a hurry, to be sent to my friends Takako and Thomas Lento with whom I shared life in Iowa, I paused for a week, then ten days, pondering. At an almost unconscious level, I recalled what Tamura said: the ideogram 線 (a line) is formed of 糸 (thread) and 泉 (fountain). That remark embodies Tamura's way of looking at things, the vision of this genuinely exceptional poet. This thought caught me by surprise, and I felt the emergence of an ephemeral spirit which he and I shared when writing poetry.

A window on America . . . why did I inscribe these words? Partly because I am conscious of American readers? But in part, perhaps, it's Tamura's imagination too . . . *(it's been a week since I wrote these words . . .)* I have been trying to trace a small path with this sentence to lead me . . . to the small window . . . to the god's gift in this poet

. . . borderless and incomparable . . . Tamura was also vaguely aware of this, and he, a former navy officer, took himself to America. *(I offer a heart-felt apology to the translator and readers.)* As I write "took himself," certain small sounds like footsteps heard from the fathomless consciousness finally begin to surface. Something like a small window led this born poet to America. "Precipice" might be a fitting word for it, as the poet himself used it in his unique way.

Perhaps very soon after the end of World War II, Tamura felt lured to civilization's precipice, which urged him to (the window on) America. This also happened almost unconsciously.

When I wrote "exceptional" at the beginning, "ex-" may have acted as a small tree-spirit . . . Now for over a month I have been tracing this path toward *Tamura Ryuichi: Life and Works*, probably the first such book in the US. I know this *(curiously faded present moment)* will be the only time I can report to American readers my discovery *(I hesitate to use such a scientific term, but I can't help it)* which is teasingly fleeting like a wind-blown, whirling leaf. My intense desire to share my thoughts with our readers is leading me down this path of *écriture* which is unusual for me as well. As of February 2011, the five-volume *Complete Works of Tamura Ryuichi* is in the process of being published, one every three months. The central part of this essay is from the piece I wrote for volume 1 of *Complete Works of Tamura Ryuichi*, published October 30, 2010. As I page through that volume I see traces of my toils and pains in writing it, just as I do in this essay. And I was struck by Tamura's last entry in this volume. It was "surprise," and that "surprise" also led me to a path I never dreamed of. This became a guiding light to my report to American readers.

> A light shines to let you see things
> capture it in words
> before it fades
>
> —Basho

In the winter of the year before last, when I was staying in a small university town in North America, a Chinese poet taught me a poem by Hu Shi. Hu Shi was born in 1891 and died in 1962, and was called the Father of modern Chinese poetry. At that time English was our only means of communication, so Hu Shi's poem was shown to me in English translation. The poem was titled "Dream and Poetry," written in 1920.

> It's all ordinary experience,
> All ordinary image.
> By chance they emerge in a dream.
> Turning out infinite new patterns.

> It's all ordinary feelings.
> All ordinary words.
> By chance they encounter a poet.
> Turning out infinite new verses.

> Once intoxicated, one learns the strength of wine.
> Once smitten, one learns the power of love;
> You cannot write my poems
> Just as I cannot dream your dreams.

My brain is imprinted with this poem which so strikingly sings the parallelism of dream and poetry. Particularly the last two lines keep coming back to me from time to time:

> You cannot write my poems
> Just <u>as I cannot dream your dreams</u>.

And now as I come across a haiku Basho wrote at the very end of his life:

> As I lie ill in bed
> on my journey
> my dream runs all about the withered field

I cannot help thinking of the dream Basho dreamed.

—Tamura Ryuichi "Basho and seven haiku
on dreams, or Dream and Poetry"[1]

I was struck with indefinable surprise when I first realized that Basho's last dream was discussed next to Hu Shi's poetry and dream, as if they are connected by a *single brilliantly shining path*. As I italicized the phrase above, my writing hand began to see Tamura's secret *(the word "secret" is too simplistic—the seed of regret leads me to another simple thought, "journey." I begin to see that Tamura, while discussing Basho's last dream, cast light on "journey" in the next line . . .)* Yes, Tamura is an incomparable traveler *(I feel like saying "un-bounded" in place of "incomparable" . . .)* and I become aware that America looms as *a channel so deep and profound, (which was italicized by this author's semi-consciousness, though the light from an outer hemisphere caused the earlier italics).*

The cover of *Complete Works of Tamura Ryuichi* quotes these three lines:

A small bird falls from the sky
A field is there
for the single bird shot down where no one was around

Those of you who have come along with me this far, reading this essay tentatively titled "A Small Window on America," might see a connection between this "field" and Basho's "withered field": what should I call it, a deep tunnel, or a well? As I walk alone down this tunnel, this well, I begin to see Tamura, this uncommon poet, from behind. I report to my unknown readers, those I meet through English translation, that I've decided the title of this piece should be "Exceptional Poet: Tamura Ryuichi." I greet you all with my eyes, as Tamura would.

*

---

[1] The underline is Yoshimasu's.

Poetry must be written . . . capturing . . . something I am going to track down . . . like invisible footprints of small animals . . . *(rather, even something similar to the shapes of sounding footsteps . . .)* capturing the moment *(necessarily and directly touching it)* as it vividly *(or)* clearly rises up to show itself. Particularly in Tamura's case *(or circumstance . . . yeah maybe close to "affair"?)* poetry is like a crater to be formed *(rather, is the form to come . . . so I repeat softly . . .)* in the universe . . . The unexpected figure of speech *boldly* bursts out . . . And I realize . . . ten minutes or so after the figure of speech has risen . . . that this crater seems also to connote something perpetually mobile such as tender leaves or bushes . . . it may have been a quiet soft voice from some trembling figure or something of the sort . . .

What is happening here . . . ? For this momentous occasion of the publication of his complete works, I initially wanted to write something stylish, light, witty, and classy in the manner of Tamura. Yet I have come to realize that "something invisible but weighty" *(is this figure of speech appropriate? I am not sure, but I hear a voice urge me on . . .)* stagnates in the area where the so-called heart entails. I felt an incorrigible want or rather wish to pull this 'invisible yet weighty' something toward the gravitational center of Tamura's poetic spirit, or toward his "inborn nature," but it was not easy to counter the resisting force . . .

Soon it will be a full twelve years since Tamura died . . . The poetry Tamura left with us, the core of his poetry . . . *(I did not want to say "heart" so I used "core" but this core was also the lead in the pencil I am using now, I realize . . .)* bears fruit . . . bears fruit? How should I put it? The way a fruit begins to form? If so, this approaches making a poem, doesn't it? . . . These thoughts begin to weigh on this short span of time *(since Tamura passed away)*, or rather maybe this is the way time works . . . I found myself, though artlessly, preposterously, and even embarrassingly, having started walking *(on June 14th, 2010, in Kagoshima, Ibusuki the next day, carrying a satchel on my back)* with *Complete Poems of Tamura Ryuichi* and several other books. Tamura Ryuichi was one who did not own things.

As this thought comes to me, an image of a precipice looms

through Tamura the medium . . . Or, a certain scenery or a tactile sense of an object this poet seems to be trying to communicate *(at this point this is beyond a simple "poet")* in his unique way *(in an invisible gesture)* . . . "A tactile sense of an object" is such a timid expression . . . have I indicated anything at all? . . . I gnash my teeth . . .

When I first thought about writing a "light, witty, stylish and classy . . ." piece on Tamura, I saw the poetic light shine in the poem below, and this essay might be simply to glean the light of this poem . . .

Also it came to me as a surprise that this essay is to be included in the first volume of his *Complete Works* . . . that means this piece will be with Tamura's earliest poetry . . . *(After his stay in Iowa, for some reason, Tamura chose to go home on Amtrak across the continent starting from Marion Station, Iowa. This is a poem coming from a gaze of his poetic mind from a train window . . .)*

> . . . dashing through the Rockies like the earth's skin
> with no birds
> no small animals
> no trees
> no grasses
>
> we've come at last to a small town called "Green River"
> the small town is dead   the only one
> young man, bare-chested, is wielding a *pickaxe*
> to demolish a deserted three-story building
> how many years on earth will it take
> to complete the demolition of that gray house?[2]

pickaxe . . . a bit of vibrato in my mouth, momentary trembling, the trembling voice . . . generating something like light, vibrating trees and pebbles in a pathway from the poet's eyes to his soul . . . this one word communicates, or rather, delivers to us the momentary shimmer of a musical instrument, and we share it and nod to it in a strange manner. In about ten lines after the above "*the golden pick-*

---

2 From "In the Dining Car."

axe" has become a poetic jewel *(I stutter a bit when I write* jewel*)* to the poet's eyes:

> still wielding a golden pickaxe
> as if I were the bare-chested young man I saw just a
>   while ago
> I drank at one dim bar after another
> where American English, Spanish,
> cigars, and perfumes were swirling
> the small town long dead
> the muddy "Green River"
> I
> kept wielding a golden pickaxe until I managed to
>   reach my solitary cell[3]

Tamura's use of italics for foreign words, or "bits of a foreign tongue" ("On My Way Home," *World Without Words*) also would be a small path to the nucleus of Tamura's poetry, but today . . . *(it's been ten days now since I started writing this. Rain, June 23, '10)* . . . I head toward something I toil to spell out but may not succeed: a reading? no, not even a message, something heartrending, sorrowful . . . I murmur "sad" and close my mouth . . . Can I spell out the verbal light shining at the periphery of woods or a grove of trees? Somehow, that scene or the light . . . *(as I ponder, I recall a scene in Ozu Yasujiro's movie "Autumn at the Kobayakawas" where the old man is lying dead and his mistress is)* sending him a breeze with a fan . . . right, she was not fanning him, but sending a breeze. That's right . . . immobile . . . "immobile" does not make sense when a breeze is being sent, yet immobile and quiet. That scene. It was like that when Tamura died. We were gathering up his ashes. I see. The trail of light in "A woman is gathering up / the ashes of someone she loves / next to her there is a violet" (Buson, translated by W.S. Merwin and T. U. Lento). Infinite traces of light, light trails are converging into the shining *pickaxe* . . . when we were collecting his ashes *(I think Buson called them bones, reading* 骨 *in the Japanese manner as "honé"*

---

[3] *ibid.*

rather than as "kotsu" in Chinese pronunciation . . .) standing in a circle, looking down, a piece of metal was tossed out there, slightly bent, maybe it was a brace implanted when he suffered a broken bone. It was as if it were a pickaxe . . . that bewildered me . . . maybe the phrase "tossed out there" hit me just as I casually wrote it down. I recalled Tamura's slightly amused voice: "You too broke your bones, huh . . . now you are a grown man." It was the morning after the Tamuras came to an Inn at Ontake, on invitation of Shinpuku Masatake . . . it was as if the shining dots of words were tossed out like broken clouds. I am now at the point where I can say to Tamura, "The bone seemed like a pickaxe," intoning Tamura's voice. Maybe this is how Tamura's poetry is to be read . . . at last I've arrived at this entry point, I should say. I am a bit fearful as well. "Tamura is one who does not own things," "a golden pickaxe," and "a metal bone," as well as "post-WWII scenery *(trails of light)*"—these phrases I jot down earlier might have been mobilized like an invisible design. Reading deep into poetry is fearsome . . . And going down the small path *(it's been two weeks already since I started writing this)* of this "invisible weight" I felt as I wrote down "with a weighty satchel on my back," and 'the golden pickaxe," . . . my essay is coming unexpectedly closer to fear and depth. This may well be a teaching of Tamura who is at the supreme and lone height of the post-WWII poetic spirit. Before it disappears I write down this teaching, maybe small yet important, which I happen to come upon, as I trace the path of his words. Then I will move to a conclusion by drawing an inference of my own as to an aspect of his secrets: why and how Tamura, alone, was able to dig a tunnel and carry the light of words to such depths of our times.

However, I wonder if we couldn't use my small pathway of this article as a guiding light to listen for some resonance or colorful tones at the depths of Tamura's poetry. I place *Complete Poems (yes like a weighty backpack . . .)* on my desk and open it . . . Yeah, this place "where no one was around" and "a field," I feel, begin to come into existence at the corner of my ears.

A small bird falls from the sky
A field is there
for the single bird shot down where no one was around[4]

... that's right, surely at this moment *(like a small bird...)*, at the corner
of an eye, the voice "A field is there" is being heard ... *(in my preface, I re-
ferred to "a tunnel" or "a well." The "field" is precisely "... where no one was around," and
"... of poetry.")* This may be why I heard something in a "place where
no one was around." Of course, this "place where no one was
around" exists in a corner of life, of trivial days ... *(the moment I turned
a corner at the back alley of Ginza holding up my umbrella, I heard Tamura whisper into my
ear, "wasn't that great you got it tossed back?" That evening [June 18, '10] I was mulling over
a few words to speak at the opening ceremony of my photo exhibit*—The Garden of Blind
Gold *is a product of almost ten years of efforts of Inagawa Masato and others, and I, the au-
thor, just tossed everything over to them ... that moment ...)* the one to toss it back
to me showed up ... the voice said, "Hey, congrats! You've done
it." That was what Tamura said at our meeting for a magazine article
to celebrate the publication of a five-volume collection of my po-
etry in 1978 *(handled by Kaneda Taro, Iida Takashi, and Aoki Ken).* His words
were somehow always quietly sitting somewhere in the corner of a
warehouse of memory ... *(The first line of "Unpleasant Picture," almost the first
poem I ever wrote, was "I had a habit of tossing things" ...)* how about that, it came
back to me like this ... *(but again, I feel fearful, and I will quote Tamura's lines;
poetry might be given life in this manner, thus I also feel as if I come in contact with wonders of
favorites. Both from* Four Thousand Days and Nights *...)*

wearing a bandage the rain went around the corner
    travelling about the sleepless city
That fall I went out to a small concert[5]

Experiencing the music resounding or sleeping in the poem
sees no boundaries. I am almost certain that the "bandage" and the

---

[4] From "A Visionary."
[5] From "The Fall," not included in this volume.

"rain" opened the door to my memory's warehouse ajar. However, I have also come to realize that "small" of this "small concert" is the nucleus of Tamura's poetry . . . the *"golden pickaxe."*

I came upon *(. . . so I felt and was convinced . . .)* the secret of the making of the tunnel in Tamura's poetry when I read remarkable passages by Kitamura Taro, who we can safely say was Tamura's life-long friend, and in Tamura's autobiographical notes I will quote later. Tamura comes alive through Kitamura's big and crystal-clear eyes:

> It was before I became friends with Tamura, though I don't recall the season, that I saw Tamura on our high school playground during recess. We were in the same class, but had not been in the same home-room. I was watching him, thinking "That's Tamura Ryuichi." I don't know why but I must say by some delicate cerebral function that I still retain that impression. Tamura was doing some sumo wrestling with someone at the time. His freshly shaven bonze head looked bluish. His facial features were neat and comely, with sharply defined eyes. His back straight, he was agile. That image of Tamura will stay with me, probably all through my life.

And the "small trip" Tamura talks about in his autobiographical notes *(from the age thirteen through eighteen)* gave him "a strange elation," which almost certainly caused him to choose to go across the American continent on Amtrak starting from Marion Station on his way home from Iowa. . . . The fountain of his poetic imagination runs through expressions such as "get off," "seven or so small bridges," "going across," and even "agile" *(though a fountain or water being agile is somewhat unusual . . . but I like it . . .)* in pieces *(this is also odd, but I like it . . .),* which amazes me:

> I entered a public high school. For the first time I was freed from the self-contained world of the geisha. I would take a city tram from Otsuka, change to another tram at Go-fukubashi, and get off at Fukagawa-Fudoson. From there

I would cross about seven or so small bridges in the Fukagawa area and go across a desolate landfill to reach my school. This small trip of one hour and a half produced a strange elation in me. Among my classmates were Kitamura Taro [a poet] and Kashima Shozo, now a scholar of American Literature.

When was it, I wonder? I was with Tamura in a taxi going through downtown. He asked the taxi to stop for a moment, and got off. For a second or two, he stood there bowing his head with his eyes closed. He quickly came back in the taxi. He just said, "My ancestors, you see." I will never forget him there at the time.

*

How about this? As I have been reviewing this essay as well as my foreword, translated by Takako Lento, I never expected this: the words "get off" and "downtown" imbue my heart. It must be that the light coming down from an extreme height has given me a momentary vision.

(Feb 9, 2011, Tokyo)

[trans. Takako Lento]

YOSHIMASU GOZO (b. 1939) is one of the most admired poets of his generation as well as a multimedia artist. In 1970, he received the Takami Jun Award for his second book of poetry, the first of his many literary awards. That year he was invited to be a poet in residence at the International Writing Program at the University of Iowa. While in Iowa, Yoshimasu corresponded extensively with Tamura, who had been a poet in residence there two years earlier. Tamura later included their correspondence in a book of essays.

Poet as Metaphor

Takako Lento

Meeting Mr. Tamura

In the late 1960's, when I was to meet Mr. Tamura for the first time, I received a postcard from him. It simply said that he would meet me at a certain station platform, that he was tall and thin, and that he would be wearing a straw hat. When I got off the train at a small station on the outskirts of Tokyo, I found him instantly. He was wearing a gardener's straw hat, and gave me a shy grin. I don't remember any formal greetings or introductions. It was as if we had grown up in the same village. He seemed to assume I shared and understood the foundations of his thought. He spoke only of matters that were divorced from the mundane details of life, but somehow deeply connected with him and his inner life. That was the beginning of our occasional association.

At that time he had spent several months in Iowa as resident poet of the International Writing Program on invitation from the poet Paul Engle. Engle was the founder and director of the program, as well as the long-time director of the Writers' Workshop at the University of Iowa. He respected Tamura as a great poet, and honored him in many different ways. Tamura wrote about his birth-day party with Paul Engle in one of his casual essays:

> I had my birthday celebrated overseas three times.
>
> One, in March of 1968, was with Professor Paul Engle, the founder of International Writing Program at the University of Iowa. That day I was absently passing time in my apartment. Suddenly Professor Engle popped in, pushed me into his car, and took me to a farm house on the outskirts of Iowa City.
>
> He announced, "Tonight we celebrate Mr. Tamura's birthday!" I was surprised because I had forgotten that it was my birthday.
>
> I call it a farm house, but around there the scale was so big you could sow seeds from an airplane. The house was a chateau. Even a Cezanne on the wall was the genuine article. About 100 people associated with the University were gathered. A "candle service" was offered. The liquor was Early Times. I was 45 years old. Boy, I was young!

In his own way Tamura enjoyed his time in Iowa. In one of his light-hearted essays, he declared his heart-felt love for Iowa City, a little town in the Corn State, in the heartland of America:

> Spring in Iowa is marvelous. Some houses have gates of forsythia. Tens of thousands of migrant birds fly in the blue sky.
>
> The downtown [of Iowa City] is small enough so I can walk in a full circle in half an hour. If you just take a step out of the town, painted houses line up connected by meandering lawns. The town has three movie houses. When one of them caught fire, curiosity seekers arrived in droves of cars, which was simply spectacular. Fire is the biggest event of this corny town. There are about ten bars. One of them is Kenny's, where they say Tennessee Williams, the author of *The Glass Menagerie*, was a regular. There are forty churches and a small jail. The regulations on alcohol are strict here because this is the home state of President

Hoover who instituted the Prohibition laws. If you want to buy whisky or brandy, you have to go out of state and buy a week's supply . . .

In this quiet university town, he enjoyed his association with many different people: distinguished visiting writers, poets and artists, as well as aspiring poets at the Writers' Workshop. He would mingle with them over a drink at his favorite bar, Donnelly's, where many years before Dylan Thomas drank when he visited Iowa City. Tamura's fondness for whisky, "the golden liquor" as he called it, was legendary. He generally would not speak English, but through a conveniently drafted interpreter, he was eloquent after a drink or two. He had an impressive understanding of the language, and its literary treasures. Many times his totally off-hand remarks would contain oblique references to T. S. Eliot, Auden, Dryden, John Donne or many others. For example, he remarked "Mercury has sunk" as he stepped out into a cold evening. Or his remarks might conjure images from mysteries by Agatha Christie or Graham Greene.

In the spring of 1971 he was on a poetry-reading tour across the U.S. on invitation of the Academy of American Poets. He observed his birthday in New York, which was the second time he "celebrated his birthday overseas:"

In 1971 at a fossilized hotel in New York I was with Tanikawa Shuntaro, Yoshimasu Gozo who flew in from Iowa, and Osawa Masayoshi, a James Joyce scholar on his way home from Dublin. They raised their glasses for me in a twin room at the hotel. The drink was Jack Daniels.

When Tamura revisited Iowa during this tour, I was teaching at the University and was also an adjunct member of International Writing Program. To commemorate Tamura's homecoming, Paul Engle had asked me to translate selected poems by Tamura. A small collection, *World Without Words* was published in time for his arrival. Tamura arrived at Iowa with his wife and his fellow poets, Tanikawa Shuntaro and Katagiri Yuzuru. Yoshimasu Gozo was a poet in residence at the International Writing Program that year. Their visit was just for a few days, but they generated the atmosphere of a re-union of distinguished Japanese poets in rural America, offering poetry readings, joining in academic and social gatherings, and gen-erally taking in Iowa. Having been drafted as an interpreter during his visit, I came to realize how sophisticated Tamura's sense of lan-guage was, often finding myself stunned by puns crossing the bar-riers of Japanese and English (and sometimes involving French). At times those untranslatable puns seemed to patter on me like rain as we walked along the main street of Iowa City. Nothing escaped his attention. Even a store name was the source of bilingual puns, sometimes lewd enough to cause his accompanying bilingual friends to blush. Yet somehow those puns were always in reference to the substance of our conversations at hand. It was an eye-opening ex-perience for me. And this experience absolutely informed my read-ing and translation of his poetry later on.

In the mid to late 70s I would visit the Tamuras in Kamakura. His house stood at the end of a narrow meandering footpath from the main road. It had a nice back yard about which he wrote in ca-sual essays: its small pond, the fate of the goldfish his wife released into it, birds coming and going, the seasonal changes of trees and flowers, and some local lore associated with the region. It was in March 1977, around his birthday, when Tanikawa, Yoshimasu, my husband and I made a visit. We had all gotten acquainted with each other in Iowa. We sat around and talked for hours. In this casual homey setting, Tamura sat straight, head high, and laughed out loud in his emphatic staccato. I vividly remember Tamura's long index finger pointing at me each time he emphasized a point in his many declarative statements, to make sure I understood his point. As I listened, I had a curious vision that his mind, if it were a sheet, was clean, starched, ironed, and folded neatly. Then I realized that words came out of his mouth as if they were lines of his poetry, pared and polished. I was struck that the classic and formal cadence in his poetry was his natural rhythm. That day he autographed his newest book, *Tamura Ryuichi, Poems 1946-76*, and handed it to me, saying, "Please translate this." He was obviously and rightly pleased with the collection, which covered his work from his earliest output after WWII to the prime of his career as a poet.

In the following years, Tamura was quite productive. After I came back to the States in the late 70s, he would send me auto-graphed copies of his new books of poetry. I would also read his casual essays and columns in Japanese newspapers and magazines. They were delightful, witty, and risqué at times, and his style was always remarkably elegant and distinctly his. He traveled widely in India, England, Scotland, and European countries on assignment from magazines and TV programs. He labeled a trip to Scotland "Researching Scotch Whisky," but his itinerary traced literary sites in Scotland. He even appeared in commercials as well as full-page newspaper ads. His tall slender figure and the angular features of his face, somewhat reminiscent of a Cherokee chief, created an impressive image of a legendary poet, as he would pose with a glass of Scotch whisky held in his long fingers.

He was a nationally beloved poet until his death in the summer of 1998. In May of that year he had published *1999*, which he had long planned to be the title of his last book of poetry, saying "I don't want to live in the 21st century. I'll leave it to you all." In his hospital room, on his last day, I was told, he asked for a piece of paper and wrote on it a few words in Japanese, which read "Death be not proud—John Donne." His wife gave him a sip of whisky through a straw. He died peacefully. It was such a fitting end.

TRANSLATING TAMURA

Impact of Linguistic Characteristics on Translations

To understand the intricacies of translating Japanese poetry into English, it may be helpful to know some general characteristics of the Japanese language:

1.   Unlike in English, word order does not determine meaning in Japanese (e.g. "A dog bit a cat." can be expressed by "dog-cat-bit" or "cat-dog-bit"). Instead, parts of speech are indicated mostly by post-positional particles. The verb is placed at the end of the sentence.
2.   The subject, object, and/or verb of a sentence can be omitted when the speaker (writer) assumes (s)he will be understood by the listener (reader), or when the speaker wants to be vague. Tamura,

however, is usually verbally specific and definitive.

3.   First person singular pronouns (I, my, me) tend to be omitted to avoid an impression of self-assertion, which has always been frowned upon in Japanese culture. Tamura, however, is rigorously explicit and specific about using these pronouns in many of his poems.

4.   Definite and indefinite articles (the, a, an) do not exist. The translator has to determine which needs to be used depending on context.

5.   Similarly, singular and plural are ambiguous, except when certain suffixes are used to specify plurality. For example, *hana* (*flower*) may be "a flower," "the flower," or "flowers," depending on context.

6.   The modifier, be it an adjective, a phrase, or the equivalent of a relative clause, precedes the word(s) it modifies. There are no relative pronouns (who, which, etc) in Japanese. The translator must supply them.

As noted above, Tamura is far more specific in his use of the language than the general practice, particularly his use of the first person pronouns. But he also takes full advantage of structural flexibilities deriving from the characteristics of Japanese to achieve his purpose.

Translating a simple statement from unspecific and structurally flexible Japanese into the rigid order of English is tricky enough. Translating poetry poses even more complex difficulties. The poet's artful manipulation of the language, compounded by cultural and literary references, sometimes results in interesting, even stunning, differences from one translation to another. Needless to say the differences derive from how translators read and internalize the original to create their English versions. As long as we believe that a poem speaks for itself, such differences are not necessarily matters of right or wrong. Readers actually might benefit from reading different versions to build their own image of a particular poem.

To illustrate the choices translators have to make, let us look at two versions of Tamura's poem "*Shi-shin*," one by Christopher Drake ("Gods of Poetry") and the other by me (my title for the same poem is "The Muse").

As I read this poem, its eight lines crystalize Tamura's view of a traditional fixed verse form and its contrast with free verse. The first line refers to Mokichi, a renowned tanka poet, Saito Mokichi (1882-1953). "Tanka" is a Japanese fixed verse form (5-7-5-7-7 syllabic rhythm) which is a millennium plus a few centuries old. Though compact, tanka can pack a lot of meaning into its 31 syllables through the poet's use of elaborately developed techniques. These techniques are as rigid, formidable, and secure as Castle walls, and Mokichi was a master practitioner and theorist of tanka.

In the first line, Tamura refers to Mokichi's *poesie* (Tamura specifically writes the word "*poesie*" in French in the middle of Japanese words). "*Poesie*" is understood among Tamura's fellow poets as poetic spirit. The protective deity of Mokichi's *poesie* resides in a traditional belief structure and environment: the temple at Asakusa, a place for the worship of the image of Kan'non (Compassionate Buddha) since the 7th century, where one can buy broiled eel, which has traditionally been considered a great source of nutrition and energy. Mokichi can count on long-established traditions, so "all he had to do was get to the temple's Thunder Gate."

Tamura, on the other hand, has to fend for himself, in a small uninsured house surrounded by great silence, because his "neurotic Muse is / always out of sorts." His precarious state as a poet is almost painful to see.

While this passage relates to Tamura's own Muse, it is also about Tamura's view of the nature of free verse. The phrase "with no fire insurance" not only indicates his current lack of security, but also echoes back to the temple in Asakusa which was reconstructed after each of the several times it was destroyed by fire over the centuries. The verbal flow in these lines is cryptic, though the tone is familiar and unassuming. Based on my reading of this poem, my translation reads as follows:

The Muse

The Muse of Mokichi's *poesie* resides in
the Compassionate Buddha and the broiled eel at
        Asakusa Temple

He trusted the castle walls of a fixed verse form, so
all he had to do was get to the temple's Thunder Gate

My neurotic Muse is
always out of sorts   with no fire insurance

in a small house and
great silence

The title "*Shi-shin*" is written in two ideograms that mean "po-
etry + god/divine being," generally points to divine inspiration, and
is often translated as the Muse of Poetry. Christopher Drake trans-
lates this title as "Gods of Poetry" and I as "The Muse."

In the body of the poem, Tamura refers to the Muse as *kami-
sama* [divine being + suffix for respect and endearment], the term
Japanese people use as a familiar but respectful address or reference
to a protective deity. This is also the word that Tamura would often
use when referring to a divine or creative inspiration: "*kami-sama*
writes the first line [of a poem] and humans write the second." The
word itself has no indication as to singular or plural. I believe this
presence is singular and deeply personal to Tamura, but Drake
chooses the plural "gods."

When we look at the structure of the first stanza, the role of
the first line is defined by the particle "*wa*," making it the topic of
the second line, which simply lists two elements: the Compassionate
Buddha and the broiled eel. If one wants to construct an English
sentence from these two lines, using the first line as the subject of
the verb "be," the subject has to be plural "gods" to agree with the
predicate (the second line), which has two elements. But since the
particle "*wa*" does not necessarily indicate that the first line is the
subject of a sentence, but simply indicates that it is a "topic" or a
"subject matter," these two lines can mean "The Muse *is associated
with or resides in* those two elements." These different readings lead
to two different translations of the first stanza, which of course af-
fect the reading of the succeeding lines.

The third and fourth stanzas pose additional challenges to
translators. "Have no fire insurance" (or "with no fire insurance"
in my version) seems to relate to the preceding line about the "ner-

vous gods" (or "neurotic Muse" in my translation), but it also modifies the next line, "small house," because an adjectival phrase precedes the noun it modifies. Who or what is "without fire insurance"? The gods/Muse or the house? Maybe both. Such dual use of an adjectival phrase is one of the familiar techniques available in traditional Japanese fixed verse forms. Because nouns have no articles attached to them in the Japanese language, and because of its generally flexible sentence construction, this type of ambiguity is relatively easy to achieve, and effectively provides an extension of content or meaning in a verse.

As to the last two lines, Tamura wrote in his short witty essay:

> The "small house and great silence" in which this "Muse" is wondrously enshrined is my rental house at Zaimoku-za, where I lived for one year and two months after I escaped from Tokyo four years ago.

In these lines he referred to his small house and great silence, but the Japanese grammar leaves room for the more general "Small houses / Large silences" in English translation.

Form of Poetry: Fixed Form vs. Free Verse

In the poem we just discussed, Tamura contrasts the reliable and steady state of fixed verse forms with the precarious state of free verse. Ooka Makoto, poet and critic, wrote:

> Here Tamura offers a light-hearted, witty, and ironical poem that consists of Tamura's banter showing his affection as well as envy for the fixed verse poet Mokichi, and Tamura's frustration with and trust, nonetheless, in his own "neurotic" Muse. The Muse of free verse, revealing a sheer precipice behind, allows only one perfected form for each attempt . . .

Ooka, a poet himself, knows the thrill and peril of having to create a form each time he writes a poem. Tamura comments that Ooka offered "generous and kind words to my poor and shabby Muse."

Tamura was keenly conscious of the form his poetry takes—not any existing form, but the form a poem takes as it asserts its own existence. In a dialogue with haiku poet Kaneko Tota, Tamura touches on the historical aspects relative to the contemporary state of free verse in Japan.

> You see, the concept of free verse would not have been born without fixed forms. In Japan, the Meiji Era, a great period in our history, enjoyed a wealth of poetic forms developed over more than a dozen centuries. Besides, we had Chinese poetic forms as well. All these provided us forms of poetry. At the same time, if I may simplify, [such forms of poetry] were interwoven with the lives of the people and ingrained in socio-cultural patterns over the years. So if one tried to get away from them, one had either to destroy or totally ignore the existing poetic forms. And of course if you destroyed traditional poetic forms, there would be no guarantee for a birth of new poetry. So again some turned to an import. Poetry, mainly European poetry in the late 19th century, which was new to Japan then, was translated into a Chinese poetic form and laid the ground for new poetry in the Meiji Era.
>
> Pre-modern Japan did not have its own original concept of free verse . . . severed from fixed forms, free verse was willfully interpreted. [In this environment] in the mid-1920s poets started talking about a poetic spirit . . . they called it *"poesie"* . . . But I believe poetry in essence demands a form for its own existence . . .

Thus Tamura rejects traditional forms as well as his immediate predecessors' "free verse," and intently pursues his own form of poetry. About his first book of poetry, he says:

> I published *Four Thousand Days and Nights*, a collection of my work from the ten years following WWII. The genesis of this book was a prose poem, titled "Etching." . . . I can say that I discovered my poetry through this poem.

And he eloquently defines what poetry is, what it does, and what shape it takes:

> The poem "Etching" was not only the genesis of *Four Thousand Days and Nights*, but also the very first poem I wrote with a furious urge to write poetry. And the fact that my furious urge produced a prose poem shows despair on my part about my poetry. I might say I was "self-conscious" about poetry. [To me] poetry is not a receptacle for manifest feelings, but a place to hide raw feelings. . . . poetry itself is not an opportunistic expression of feelings. It makes totally unspecific amorphous feelings distinct and clear. It also makes them visible and clearly audible. In other words, it gives them a well-defined shape as an "object." It is an intrinsic construct reinforced within by means of rhythms, colors, images, and delicate interactions among words. Poetry is not created by any specific concept or vague emotions. We need to keep in mind the obvious principle, "Poetry is made of words." And it is by means of a construct called poetry that concepts and emotions are generated. A poet, through writing, thereby creating a shape with words, makes visible emotions and concepts which have not yet been separable and clear in his own mind. Once that is done, his concept shakes up its reader's total sensibilities by its freshness and energy, and his emotions profoundly affect the reader's intellect by means of the concept's inherent logic and osmotic force.

In Tamura's view each piece of poetry must be a unique presence in its own form, clarifying a yet-to-be-defined idea. It should even physically shock the reader's psyche into awakening to its significance. Tamura's mission was to capture his "furious urge" in words to construct this poetry. He succeeded in his mission from the first book of poetry he published.

Influences on Tamura's style are multifold. Born in 1923 and raised as the first son of a restaurateur in a small pleasure district on the outskirts of Tokyo, he grew up surrounded by old-fashioned traditional arts and customs. Traditional rhythmic cadences were in the air as he was growing up. But at the same time this period coincided with the rapid influx of European modernist movements to Japan. As Tamura says:

> The year before I was born, a whole lot of literature such as James Joyce, Marcel Proust, and T. S. Eliot's *The Waste Land* came into the world. And in the mid-1920s those cultural influences arrived on the shore of Japan. With that, in the field of poetry, literary movements such as Poetry and Poetics led by Haruyama Yukuo blossomed. Of course along with French modern literature, works of artists such as Picasso, Dali, Chirico, and Miró were introduced to Japan one after another. The Cubist and Futurist movements— all those just burst into Japan all at once.

He was precocious, and he felt stifled by the aging tradition-bound culture around him. He felt liberated when he began to commute to high school outside his hometown. He was twelve years old. He quickly involved himself in the literary activities of young aspiring poets. He writes in his autobiographical notes:

> 1935-40
> I entered a public high school. For the first time I was freed from the self-contained world of the geisha. I would take a city tram from Otsuka, change to another tram at Go-fukubashi, and get off at Fukagawa-Fudosan. From there I would cross about seven bridges in the Fukagawa area and go across a desolate landfill to reach my school. This little trip of one hour and a half produced a strange elation in me. Among my classmates were Kitamura Taro [a poet] and Kashima Shozo, now a scholar of American Literature. . . . In my junior or senior year, through Kitamura Taro's intro-

duction, I joined a coterie poetry magazine *Le Bal* edited by Nakagiri Masao. Also around that time I joined *Shin-Ryodo* [*New Country*] . . . By virtue of joining *Le Bal* I got to know some poets who were three or four years older than I and already college students. . . . Given the stirring elation I gained from just a 1.5 hour tram trip from the third-rate world of the geisha, my readers can easily imagine how intellectually stimulated and excited I was by meeting these people, and by coming in contact with their conversations and discussions, their poetry and their essays. Everything was new to me, and everything made me curious. These poets were influenced mainly by the European literature of post-WW I and the associated literary movements of the era. I honestly felt that I had discovered a horizon so far unknown. As I entered High School, the 2-26 (1936) incident [a failed military coup d'état, which resulted in stronger military control over politics in Japan] took place. Then the China Incident. Japan's military activities kept expanding to finally involve the whole of China, and World War II started in Europe. In 1940 I read "The Waste Land" by T.S. Eliot in the English original for the first time. In 1938 I had read part of "The Waste Land" in a stiff Japanese translation in the August issue of *New Country*. . . . As I read the original,

> Summer surprised us, coming over Starnbergerse
> With a shower of rain;

I discovered that what "surprised us" was "Summer" and learned some syntax that was unavailable in the Japanese language . . .

His exposure to European modernism was through Japanese translations, but Tamura was trained in English and Western culture thanks to his high school principal, who was intent on broadening his students' perspective. This is especially remarkable since English was labeled as the "enemy language" as Japan went into WWII. Tamura absorbed what was made available to him from European modernist movements. He was in his early teens when he started writing poetry in a pretentiously modernistic vein.

Tamura stopped writing during the war, but when the war ended, facing the devastation and despair in the war-torn landscape all around him, he internalized the Waste Land as his mindscape. At this point Tamura started to be a conscious poet, speaking with his own voice and style, soaring remarkably above the old traditions as well as the imported modernism. Tamura himself rejects his youthful pre-war poetry as "etudes," and when we discuss his poetry, we refer to his post-WWII poetry.

TAMURA'S STYLE—VOICE AND DICTION

When we read Tamura's poetry, particularly his early poems, a sense of tautness grips us. Each word is specifically selected and placed. The lines they form are clean, crisp and tight, which generates a haunting nervous tension. Firmly rejecting traditional emotion-driven diction, cadences, and rhythms, his lines are starkly bare and full of metaphors. The element of surprise also captivates our attention: in his choice of words themselves, in the relationships among words and lines, in the ideas presented through them, or in the sharp breaks between stanzas, or even lines. The voice is intense and declarative, but curiously neutral, as if to preempt empathy. In other words, Tamura created a shockingly new poetry. His friend Kitamura Taro wrote about Tamura's earliest creations, his prose poems:

> During the latter half of the 1940s, after WWII, Tamura wrote a series of prose poems. Each time he wrote a piece, he read it to me in his penetrating and clear voice. Even though it was in prose, it had a unique rhythm, which was quite pleasing as I listened to it. When he finished reading he would break into loud and cackling nervous laughter. I would laugh with him, having been impressed and moved by the poem. In every one of those poems, the last line gave me a shock, such as "He, namely the man I have begun to tell you about, killed his father when he was young. That autumn his mother went beautifully mad" ("Etching"), or

"What a beautiful face. He trusts the world like a flower" ("Sunken Cathedral"). As I laughed with him, I clearly understood his incomparable joy of discovering such beautiful music in his inconsolable despair.

But even with this often clinically clean style, the traditional air Tamura breathed during his childhood is assimilated into his poetics in a subtle and elegant manner. Of the traditional popular art forms, Tamura was particularly fond of *rakugo*, a form of comic storytelling presented in a cozy theatre by a storyteller sitting alone in the middle of a stage with no props. Each story is a slice of common life, delivered as lively banter among its characters, interspersed with exquisite pauses. It always ends with a line that comes as an epiphany revealing the truth behind the story in a flash. Some point out that Tamura's fondness for this storytelling art shows particularly in his later writings. That is evident in his delightful light essays. Certainly we see it also in his poetry, and not exclusively in the later work. Take, for example, "Lieberman Goes Home." It is witty, loquacious, and funny. Compared to poems such as "Four Thousand Days and Nights" or "October Poem" the differences are astounding. But both kinds of poem are uniquely Tamura's own. And as Kitamura Taro pointed out, each of Tamura's earliest prose poems had a shocking final line—reminiscent of the conclusions in *rakugo*. It's a pattern that we see throughout his career, though it's more apparent in the later work, which tends to be in more relaxed and colloquial style.

POEM AS A METAPHOR

In a discussion on poetry with a haiku poet, Tamura said,

You see, poets use various figures of speech, in many different forms. But they are not simply trying to represent something with figures of speech. Instead they are using them in the hope of discovering a paramount metaphor. . . . When I say "the world without words," I am far from denigrating or ignoring words, but I am saying how great it would be if a poem could materialize a world where figures of speech simply could not intervene, in other words, if a poem can make its whole self into a genuine metaphor.

Tamura is speaking of his ideal in terms of metaphor here: creating a poem to be an entity, an absolute crystallization of the poetic spirit, that directly speaks to its reader on its own terms. Let us again look at "Etching," "the very first poem [he] wrote with a furious urge to write poetry." Its first passage gives us the cityscape the protagonist faced, recalling one he saw in a German etching. In the second passage he tells us of his resolute rejection of his father. He buries what his father represents, namely, his stifling hometown and its outmoded mores. He also tells us of his mother's condition, perhaps signifying a crazed post-WWII motherland. Notably a possible transition to dawn is hinted at and his mother's madness is perceived as "beautiful," suggesting hope of renewal. As we read this we stand speechless, seeing devastation, rejection, despair, and a faint glimmer of hope in front of our eyes. But what moves us in this poem is not necessarily tied to the regional realities of the post-WWII Japan and Tamura's individual perceptions of and despair over them. This poem has achieved the status of being a single metaphor to convey Tamura's "concepts and emotions," freed from the constraints of time and space. We recall Tamura's words, "And it is *by means of* a construct called poetry that concepts and emotions are generated." In its perfection, poetry exists on its own terms and speaks in a universal language. He kept his sight on this ideal throughout his career as a poet, no matter what style his poems took.

(2011)

TAKAKO LENTO, a poet, translator, and coeditor of this volume, has taught at universities in Japan and the U.S. She holds an MFA in poetry and translation from the Iowa Writer's Workshop, and her publications include book-length Japanese translations of American writers as well as English translations of, and essays on, Japanese poets. She is a regular contributor on Japanese poetry to Poetry International Web. Her *Tanikawa Shuntaro: The Art of Being Alone—Poems 1952-2009*, translations with a critical introduction, is forthcoming from Cornell East Asia Series.

Books by Tamura in English translation (all in limited availability):

Tamura Ryuichi. *Dead Languages: Selected Poems, 1946-1984*. Trans. Christopher Drake. Santa Fe: Katydid Books, 1984.

Tamura Ryuichi. *Poetry of Ryuichi Tamura*. Trans. Yumiko Tsumura and Samuel Grolmes. Palo Alto: CCC Books, 1998.

Tamura Ryuichi. *Tamura Ryuichi, Poems: 1946-1998*. Trans Yumiko Tsumura and Samuel Grolmes. Palo Alto: CCC Books, 2000.

Tamura Ryuichi. *World Without Words*. Trans. Takako Uchino Lento. Woodstock, NY: Ceres Press, 1971.

About the Series:

Volumes in the Unsung Masters Series are published once a year by Pleiades Press (as long as funding allows) and feature work by, and essays on, unjustly neglected or out-of-print writers. Each volume in the series is distributed free to *Pleiades* magazine subscribers with the summer (June) issue. Unsung Masters Series book are also available through Small Press Distribution.

Volume 1, *Dunstan Thompson: On the Life & Work of a Lost American Master*, edited by D. A. Powell & Kevin Prufer, 2010

Volume 2, *Tamura Ryuichi: On the Life & Work of a 20th Century Master*, edited by Takako Lento & Wayne Miller, 2011

Volume 3, on Nancy Hale, edited by Dan Chaon & Phong Nguyen, will be published in 2012

Volume 4, on Russell Atkins, edited by Michael Dumanis & Kevin Prufer, will be published in 2013

Series editors: Wayne Miller, Phong Nguyen, & Kevin Prufer